A WITNESS TO A
NON-HAPPENING

Memoirs of a Holocaust Survivor

Saul Birnbaum

ISBN: 1545402914
ISBN-13: 9781545402917
Library of Congress Control Number: 2017906203
CreateSpace Independent Publishing Platform
North Charleston, South Carolina

CONTENTS

PART ONE

1939–1945

PREFACE

The limousine pulled up in front of the house, and the whole family stepped out. The whole family minus one. Dorika was left behind at the New Montefiore Cemetery, way out on Long Island. A year and a half of living hell. Doctors, hospitals, cobalt treatment, and chemotherapy did not help. She died on December 29, 1974, at the age of forty-nine.

As Jewish law requires, a bottle of water was prepared at the door to wash our hands before we entered the apartment. The mirrors were covered with white sheets. Low cardboard boxes and chairs were scattered around the living room for the mourners to sit on during the seven days of *shiva*. The table was heaped with food; we had not eaten all day. A lot of people were at the cemetery.

We sat down—that is, my two sons (Arthur and Howard), Dorika's sister Lili, and I—and that's how we spent the seven days of shiva. I was exhausted after the past three days. On Saturday, I was notified that the end was near. I spent all day and night, Saturday and Sunday till noon in her hospital room. At noon, she died. Arrangements had to be made with the hospital and the funeral chapel; then there was the funeral itself.

Death was nothing new to me. I'd seen more than my share of it between the years 1939 and 1945. Family, friends, and other people whom I'd known had died before my eyes. Nothing affected me as much as this. The visitors left, and we went to sleep. The next day, after a small breakfast, we sat down again. That is when I started to tell my sons about the events that had led to our coming to America.

PROLOGUE—THE VOYAGE

"America! America!"

The scream woke us up that morning of January 17, 1949, and almost everybody on the *Marine Flasher* was suddenly well again. For ten days and nights, seasickness had prevailed. The dining rooms had been almost empty ever since we'd entered the English Channel. The first evening, all the passengers had come down for dinner. The tables were covered with white linen and piled with food. None of us had seen that much food since 1939. In the center of the room, the main table was filled with a dazzling array of delicacies. A special corner was set up for those among us who ate only kosher food.

There were four people to a table, and a waiter served us the food. It seemed as if the plates in front of us were never emptied. As soon as we cleared the plates, they were immediately replaced with others just as loaded. We, the people who hadn't had a decent meal for over ten years, ate as if we were preparing to hibernate for the next eleven. Some of us were curious to find out how to stop the ship, because we wanted to spend a few weeks in that kind of luxury. After dinner, we enjoyed movies, dancing, and entertainment. Later, the gentle rolling of the ship lulled us into a restful sleep.

We entered the English Channel during the night. The waters were rough, as usual, and everyone became seasick. Luggage was tossed from one side of the cabin to the other. I just tied myself down to my bunk and returned to sleep, only to be woken a little while later by a voice telling me that my wife was seasick. The *Marine Flasher* was an army transport and now a DP (displaced persons) boat. A ten-thousand-ton boat isn't particularly heavy, and in this storm, the boat was being heaved and thrown this way and that. It wasn't easy for those of us aboard. The men were on the lower deck, the women and children on the upper decks. The stench of vomit hung heavily in the air. I tried to get up, but my head began to spin at every attempt. Somehow, I managed to get dressed while lying down, and then I ran up the stairs to my wife's cabin. Dorika was really sick. I had never seen her in such a terrible state. I took her up to the main deck lounge, where she and many others remained throughout the whole voyage.

Four of us had been at our table the first evening there, but from the following morning on, I was the only one. I made a deal with the other people—I'll eat for them, and they'll vomit for me. Next to my bunk was a paper container on which someone had written, "Here slept a Pole from Warsaw who wasn't sick even once." Under that I wrote, "Here slept a Jew from Przemysl, and he wasn't sick, either." Nothing exciting happened other than a few more storms and a few nice days. Then, early one morning, we were all awakened by screaming from above. We raced to the upper decks, and in the morning mist we saw our first sight of America. The boat trip had taken only eleven days, but for me the whole voyage had taken ten years...

CHAPTER 1

A SHORT HISTORY OF MY TOWN

I was born in a middle-size town in Poland by the name of Przemysl, located in the picturesque valley of the River San. The river divided the city into two parts: Przemysl and Zasanie ("Behind the San"). Przemysl (the old city) was built on the eastern bank of the river, with streets leading up toward Summit Street, the highest point in our town. Zasanie, on the western bank, was built on the flatlands that stretched for miles into the countryside.

The most important feature of our town was the immense park, called the *zamek* (castle) for the ruins of an old castle located there. Beautifully manicured flower beds, extensive nature walks, wide benches for resting, and dense woods to wander made our park a real Garden of Eden. On weekends, the whole population of the city migrated to the park. I still have happy memories of the days I spent with my family there. On Saturday afternoons, many Jewish families congregated in the picnic area. Sitting on blankets on the grass, families enjoyed the warm weather, eating, drinking, and singing. At sunset, they conducted prayers of *mincha* and *maariv* (evening prayers) and then went to their homes.

The other memorable thing about our town was the river. In the summer this was our beach. I spent the weekends swimming, sunbathing, and boating with my friend Nusiek, his girlfriend Poldzia, and my girlfriend Chaycia. We were denied all that fun during the last years before the war. The Endeks (the National Democrat Party), a very anti-Semitic organization, would initiate fights at the beach. Many Jewish boys were killed as a result of those riots. In winter, the river served as a skating rink, where we had lots of fun. In the spring, the gentle river, swollen by the melting snow from the Carpathian Mountains, changed into a raging killer. It was fascinating to watch the houses, trees, and the carcasses of farm and wild animals rush by. On our side of town, the banks escaped any damage, but Zasanie, with its low banks, was flooded every spring.

My family—which consisted of my father (Asher), my mother (Esther), my brother Beniek, my sister Frieda, my grandmother Pesla, and I, Siolek (my

Polish name), the firstborn—lived in the Jewish section of town (Zydowskie miasto). My father was the owner of a very prosperous grocery store, with my mother helping in the store and my grandma taking care of the house. The children attended school, helping out in the store on our free time.

Przemysl was a town of seventy thousand inhabitants, of whom seventeen thousand were Jews, mostly small businessmen and artisans. The Jews had lived in the town since the year 1040. Life for the Jews was sometimes good under the protection of the kings and sometimes brutal, especially when the Cossacks, under the leadership of Chmielnicki, pillaged the towns, killing hundreds of people each time.

As a young boy, I often wandered with my friends in the undergrounds of the old fortifications surrounding our town. Because the town was a very important Austrian military fort during World War I, the Austrians fought many battles against the Russians for its possession.

In 1961, our town, together with the country, celebrated its thousandth year of existence. The first documents to show that Jews lived in the town dated from between 1020 and 1040. King Casimir the Great (1310–1370) invited Jews escaping from the pogroms in Western Europe to live there. He gave them special privileges, had a synagogue built (the "old shul"), and engaged in business and trade with the Jews.

When Poland was divided between Russia, Germany, and Austria in the seventeenth century, our town, as part of Galicia, came under Austrian rule. As noted above, our town became a very important fort during the First World War, when it was captured by the Russians and then recaptured by the Austrians. Many of the inhabitants died of hunger and epidemics during the fighting. The first thing the Russians did when they arrived was to expel the Jews, but when the Austrians recaptured the town in 1915, life for the Jews returned to normal.

CHAPTER 2

WAR!

In 1939, my uncle Izaak mailed me an affidavit to come to America. My quota number was supposed to come up in 1940, but an Austrian housepainter by the name of Adolph Hitler stopped me from leaving Europe. The year 1939 was a very tumultuous year. Czechoslovakia disappeared from the map, and Hitler was ready to swallow Poland. The whole country was prepared for war. Air-raid tests, with sirens sounding a few times a day, made everybody run for cover. Everyone was busy digging trenches. Edward Rydz-Smigly, the Polish marshal, said that "We won't give even a fistful of our soil to the Germans." All the eligible boys were drafted into the army, and the younger ones became air wardens. Hitler demanded the Polish Corridor, which stretched from Germany to Prussia across the narrow strip of land given to Poland in 1918 after Germany lost World War I.

Our town seemed far away from Germany, but the war frenzy was catching up with us. People were seeing German spies on every corner. A priest, a nun, or a bum not walking the right way all came under suspicion. Often it turned out to be true. There was a dentist who could pull teeth without pain, for example. Just by touching around the bad tooth, he was able to extract it with his fingers. One day he was apprehended while taking pictures of a military installation from his office where he was pulling teeth. There was also an old man who always pulled a wagon loaded with rags and garbage around town. He, too, was arrested when the police found radio and photo equipment in his possession. In school, we were taught how to wear gas masks, and the pace of digging trenches kept increasing. Every empty lot and every backyard was dug up. By the end of September, Russia and Germany signed a non-aggression pact, and on September 29, Hitler demanded the city of Danzig.

It was vacation time, and as usual, our family went away to the country for the summer. Father stayed home and took care of the grocery store. We, the children, had a wonderful time. It was the best summer in my memory. One evening a man came and told us to pack up and get ready to go home.

The situation was very serious, and father was worried. We came home that same night, just in time. On September 1, 1939, Hitler invaded Poland. It was a Friday, a market day. A very busy day in our town. All the farmers from the surrounding villages would come into town to sell their products.

The stores were full of people, and the streets were crowded. The marketplace was called Targowica. It was rather a large area, surrounded by stores and bars. The market was overflowing with people. The noise was ear-shattering, the sellers calling out their goods, the cows and horses mooing and neighing.

Sirens started to wail around eleven in the morning, but no one paid attention until the air wardens started to chase the people away. Many of them went into the cellar of a five-story building across the street; a few farmers went into a bar in the same building. Then the planes came. The sounds of explosions shook the city. People came running from where the bombs had fallen, telling horrible stories. Near the market was the town's electrical plant. A bomb that was intended for the plant hit a building a few blocks away from where people had taken shelter. The house was cut in half. It looked like a doll house with exposed rooms. Tables, chairs, and other items of furniture were still standing intact. All that was left of the other half was a pile of bricks, with an unknown number of people buried underneath. Only then did we realize that this was war. The time for tests was over; from now on, a siren meant death and destruction. For us, the youngsters, it was something new and exciting, but our parents knew what war meant. World War I had ended just twenty years before, and our town had played a very large part in that war. The soldiers of 1914 still remembered. The old people of Fort Przemysl still remembered. We always heard of the hard times, the hunger, the sickness, and the death during the war. My father, who was an Austrian soldier, fought from 1914 to 1917. He was then taken as a prisoner of war by the Russians. At the war's end in 1917, when he was freed from the camp, he met my mother, a Litvak (a Lithuanian Jew), and he a Galizianer (a person from Galicia). They fell in love and got married.

Przemysl was a town where Jews were never welcomed. Well, almost never, if you think back to King Casimir the Great. The Jews had lived in this town for hundreds of years—sometimes well, sometimes in danger of their lives—but somehow they always survived. Our town had seventeen thousand Jews; the other fifty-three thousand or so were Poles and Ukrainians. A few rich Jews lived there, but most were poor: tailors, shoemakers, and store owners. The town had a few Polish stores, but the farmers preferred to buy from the Jews.

Then sometime in 1939, a Polish priest (*trzeciak*) was instrumental in passing a law against the kosher slaughter of animals. He called for the boycott of Jewish stores. Following the example of Germany, Poland instituted quotas for Jews in the universities. Then the pogroms started. Pogroms were the enjoyment of the masses. Looking back, it was just children's play compared to what the Germans had in store for us. Well, let's get back to the war at hand.

As I said, it was September 1, 1939. The first bombs were dropped on our town. For fourteen days we had visits from German planes, sometimes dropping a bomb but more often just passing to or from a bombing mission. So started a *Blitzkrieg* that lasted several years. On September 3, Britain and France declared war on Germany. This, we thought, was the end of the war. Surely the Germans wouldn't be able to fight on two fronts. But then a curious thing happened. Neither country made any attempt to go to Poland's aid. The news was bad. The German army couldn't be stopped. Poland had an army almost as big as Germany's, but it lacked the weapons for modern warfare. The Polish cavalry was no match for the German tanks, and the few old-fashioned planes could not dream of fighting the *Luftwaffe* (air force). Our town was getting ready for a siege. "Maybe we'll stop them on the River San," said the Polish soldiers, "just like we stopped the Russian army with the 'miracle on the Vistula' in 1917."

In the meantime, the Polish army was running away. Soldiers without shoes or uniforms were passing through our town on their way from the front. It had been only fourteen days since the war had started, and the Germans were nearing our town. The two bridges were mined, and the town was ready to fight. Father decided to take my mother, sister, and brother to a farm outside town. I stayed home and almost left with my friends, who headed toward the Russian border. The next day, my family came back tired and scared. The Ukrainians had threatened them. They said that as soon as the Germans came in, they would kill all the Jews. So there was nothing to do but return home.

CHAPTER 3

THE FIRST BATTLE FOR PRZEMYSL

Friday, August 15, was a day of waiting. A deadly quiet fell over our town. Everybody was waiting for the unknown. The defense was in the hands of the students of a military school. By noon, one bridge had gone up in the air. Our houses were only two city blocks from the bridge, and it sounded as if the whole neighborhood were coming down. Everyone ran from the houses when the buildings started to shake. I was running into the street when something dropped in front of me. Picking it up, I burned my fingers. It was a piece of steel from the bridge that had flown toward me. One inch farther, and that piece would have gone through my skull. I kept it as a lucky charm. But they took it away from me in 1943, in one of the concentration camps.

The first German artillery shells hit our town late in the afternoon. Our defenders only had small arms against the Germans' heavy artillery. It was like a flea trying to stop an elephant. No one was in command. The big guns were pouring steel from across the river, and from our side, we could hear sporadic machine-gun fire and single shots. I really don't know what held the Germans back. Maybe it was the demolished bridge, or maybe they were waiting for the Polish soldiers to escape. Anyway, the shooting kept up until late into the night. In our neighborhood, the local liquor monopoly had a big warehouse loaded to the rafters with all kinds of alcoholic beverages. What had to happen, happened.

The soldiers broke down the doors, and a free-for-all ensued. Alcohol started to flow in the street. We came running with pots and pails to fill up and take the liquor home. Everyone was drunk: the soldiers, the children, the adults, and even the dogs and cats. Night came, and a deadly silence fell over the city. The second bridge across the river, used only by the railroad, was still intact.

The Germans came across it on Saturday morning. It was Rosh Hashanah, the Jewish new year, but no one was in a holiday mood. Our defenders disappeared, and the long-awaited miracle on the River San never occurred. We stayed home, but many Jews dressed in holiday finery, went to their places of worship. After all that shooting, it was very quiet. Then we heard shouting and running. We knew that the devil had arrived.

CHAPTER 4

TWO WEEKS IN HELL

It is said that the devil isn't as black as they paint him, but in two short weeks, we found out that they did not paint him black enough. So, on Rosh Hashanah, we got our first taste of life under the German occupation as Nazi soldiers spread terror throughout the Jewish community. They came into our homes and took all the males, old and young, to work. We had to build a bridge over the River San so that the German armored divisions could cross it. As I said, the Jews were dressed in holiday clothes, ready to go to the temple. But by noon we were dirty, and our clothes were torn to shreds. We had to carry heavy boards from distant lumberyards and cut them to size for the bridge. Many older Jews were taken from the temples wearing the *tallisim* (pure wool prayer shawls), and the Nazis made them work; meanwhile, the Polish population looked on with happy smiles on their faces. There was no stopping under the watchful eyes of the Germans. We were rushed and beaten. The tempo was murderous. We had to run all the time. They kept on yelling "Schnell, schnell, verfluchte Juden!" ("Faster, faster, damned Jews!") I was able to escape around noon, but the others worked until late at night. After the bridge was finished, the German army started to roll through our city. Never have I seen so many cars, trucks, tanks, guns, horses, and killing machinery.

The ten days between Rosh Hashanah and Yom Kippur were real hell for the Jews, who were hunted like animals in the streets and taken to workplaces from which they never returned. They were later found in mass graves, shot by the Nazis. A few of my friends and I were hiding in a third-floor room in our house that my mother kept locked from outside with a padlock. She opened it only in the evenings, when we could go home for the night. We could hear the soldiers banging on the doors, so we kept quiet, afraid to breathe. The Germans did not let up in their terror tactics. They went from house to house and from store to store, taking everything that appealed to them.

They stopped Jews in the streets, emptied their pockets, and then beat them just for the fun of it. On

Thursday morning, my father was taken away with many other men to work. We didn't know about it until our mother let us out in the evening. Looking through the windows, I felt sick when I saw what the German beast was doing to the old men. Men with white beards, dressed in black silk coats, were forced to pull heavy wagons, pick up horse manure with bare hands, and load it onto the wagons. The Poles and Ukrainians were standing around, having fun. The Germans were using bayonets to cut the old men's beards, sometimes with the skin still attached, cutting swastikas on the old men's heads.

I often wondered how our mother felt, with our father taken away and my brother and I hidden in a room from which we could be taken away at any moment. Our father came back by late afternoon—the only one of the whole group. He told us a story that sounded like something out of the Arabian Nights. All the men were led into a large room filled with SS (Schutzstaffel) men. Behind the desk sat a gray-haired German officer who started to ask them, "Were any of you soldiers in the last war? On which side were you fighting?" My father and two other men told him that they had been in the Austrian army. Papa was drafted in 1914, spent two years on the front, and in 1916, as noted earlier, was taken as a POW by the Russians. He spent two years in POW camps in Siberia. The other two men were drafted in 1916. One of them was sick, so he never went to the front. The other one was on duty in town.

The German then gave back my father's ID papers and wallet and said to the others, "Dieser Mann hat schon genug gearbeitet, so er kann nach Hause gehen, und ihr wird ein paar Tage arbeiten und dann nach Hause gehen." ("This man has worked enough in his life, so he may go home, but you will work a few days first, and then you will go home.") None of the other men ever came back. They were found shot to death in a mass grave outside town. This happened in retaliation for Jews shooting at German soldiers from a window, which was untrue. I remember my friend Moniek, whose father was also killed, saying *kaddish (prayers)* on Yom Kippur and asking, "Why, why, why was he killed?" Two years later, Moniek himself was shot by the Gestapo for taking two clothes hangers from the workshops.

For two weeks after Rosh Hashanah we were hunted like wild animals. The Nazis didn't let up in their persecution of the Jews. It seemed that this would be the end of us. No Jew was safe in the street; many times they broke into Jewish homes and took anything they liked. German soldiers took expensive items, leaving a receipt that no Jew was ever going to claim.

We heard rumors that the Russian army had crossed the eastern border and was advancing into

Poland. On September 23, as I mentioned, Russia and Germany signed a non-aggression pact and arranged to divide Poland between them. The demarcation line ran along the Rivers San and Bug. As the reader will recall, the River San divides our town into two parts: Przemysl and Zasanie. Przemysl, the part of town where we lived, was to be occupied by the Russians, and Zasanie by the Germans. In those days, every piece of red cloth available was being sewn into flags. Everyone was waiting impatiently for the "red messiah," as the religious Jews called the Russians. In the meantime, the Nazis didn't stop their dirty work. The looting and killing went on, and no one believed it would ever end. So Yom Kippur came and went. The Russian army was nearing our town, and we hoped the Germans would not pull one of their last-minute surprises. On Friday night, an explosion woke us up. Looking out from the window, we could see flames not far from us. The Germans hurled firebombs into King Casimir the Great's old synagogue and set the new temple on fire. The Germans would not permit the firemen to put out the fires, and they cut their water hoses. The Nazis left by morning, and we tried to save what remained of the temple. The fire was out by eight, but the temple was in ruins. I was soaked to the skin after working the whole morning, trying to save the adjoining building. The streets were full of people with smiling faces by this time, finally free from the devil. I went home and was told that the Red Army was already on the outskirts of town. After washing and dressing, I walked into town, which now had a holiday look. Red flags and flowers were everywhere. People were singing and dancing in the streets. The main street, Mickiewicza, was lined with people, dancing and waiting for the Russians.

We suddenly heard the sound of German singing. The last detachment of German soldiers was marching out. Everyone started to spit at them and curse them, but they just marched by, singing and not paying any attention to us. Now we knew that the worst was over.

CHAPTER 5

THE FIRST LIBERATION

The people stood along the street, impatiently awaiting the arrival of the Russian army. Somebody came running and screamed, "The Russian tanks are coming!" All of a sudden, silence enveloped us. The masses of people were listening for the sound of motors. And then the long-awaited moment came. The tanks were rumbling down the street. They were all covered with flowers. As soon as they stopped, we were on top of them. We were hugging and kissing the soldiers. The picture is almost beyond description. Old bearded Jews came out, carrying the holy Torah and welcoming our liberators. There was more singing and dancing. People shouted, "No more hiding!" There was no end to our happiness. We felt like human beings again.

Many of the soldiers were dressed in civilian clothes. When we asked why they were out of uniform, they answered, "We are not soldiers; we are factory workers. When we were asked to come and help liberate our brothers in west Ukraine, we didn't even say goodbye to our families but went straight from work into Poland."

Because it was the Jewish holiday Sukkoth, and we'd been unable to build *sukkoths* (tabernacles) when the Germans were around, whoever was able began building now. It was really a very happy holiday. We felt free again after being in hell for two weeks. Across the river, the German beast was sitting and waiting.

Life was returning to normal. The Russians were opening government stores, but small private stores were also permitted to operate. We opened our grocery store again and sold our old stock and anything else we could buy. Internal passports were given only to those who had lived in Przemysl proper before September 1939. All others—and there were many, even those who lived in Zasanie—were considered refugees and had to leave our town. Not everyone left. Many went into hiding. Others took the names of people who were missing so that they could obtain passports. For the next few months, nothing worth mentioning happened but for one notable exception.

On November 30, 1939, Russia invaded Finland. The Russian bear did not find the going as easy as the Germans had found it in Poland. It took them five months, until March 1940, to force the Finns to surrender. The Russian losses were extremely high, which we used to joke about.

All was quiet on the western front during the winter of 1939/40. The refugees who did not leave town were told to register. Whoever wanted to go back to the other side would get permits and be able to do so. The others would get passports but would have to move at least one hundred miles from the border. In the meantime, no one bothered them. Everyone was trying to make a living. There was a joke that went like this. "When the Russians came, they fulfilled everyone's wishes. The Poles wanted businesses to be in Polish hands, so they sold their possessions to be able to buy food. The Jews wanted government jobs, so they gave them jobs as street sweepers. The Ukrainians wanted a free Ukraine, which they could buy at any newsstand for ten kopeck." (This refers to the newspaper *Free Ukraina*.)

The Russians brought with them a lot of rubles and were buying everything they could lay their hands on. I saw a soldier buy a meat grinder, turn the handle, and wonder why it didn't play. They bought watches by the dozen. The Russian wristwatch was as big as a pocket watch with straps added.

Our small watches, even a Mickey Mouse watch, was a big deal for them. We saw some Russians wearing three watches on each arm, and even some on their ankles. A few Russians were sold empty watch cases with live flies inside. When they put the case to their ears, they could hear the flies buzzing, which they mistook for ticking. Their wives bought nightgowns and wore them as dresses. The men bought tuxedos with top hats and wore them with their boots.

The winter of 1939 was very tough for me. My father was a businessman, and even though I worked for the government, my passport stated "Supported by a businessman." That made me a second-class citizen, which meant that I was vulnerable to all kinds of harassment. When the snow fell, which was very often, I and many like me were forced to clear it. The militia stopped people in the street, took their passports away, and told them to report for snow clearing. We were paid very little. We had to work three or four days until our passports were returned to us, until the next snowfall came and we had to do it again.

I got a job delivering bread from a bakery to the government stores. I had to leave home at 3:00 a.m. On my way to work, I could see people lining up for their bread rations. It was cold and dark, and the delivery was hours off. At the bakery, we had to wait for the horses and the wagon (we had no trucks) to come. When they arrived, we started to load the wagon with hot bread. The bread was black and half-raw; it was never well done. Despite the lack of food, we had to take the bread back many times because people refused to buy it. The bread was not thrown away but put back into the dough and baked again. The stores in the suburbs sold the bread to the farmers, who fed it to their pigs. In the summer of 1940, I gave my job to my younger brother and went to work at the railroad-repair shops.

CHAPTER 6

A SURPRISE GUEST

One day in December 1939, a friend of mine who worked as a guard in the city prison came to our home and told me that a prisoner there by the name of Siolek Rubin from Rzeszow claimed to be our relative. The man had been caught by the Russian border patrol while crossing the River San, which was now the German-Russian border. For the sum of five hundred rubles, my friend was able to free Siolek from prison.

He was indeed the son of our father's sister. His family had immigrated to Palestine in 1937, and he stayed behind to liquidate their jewelry business and was caught by the fast-moving German army. The situation was getting desperate, so he decided to leave for the Russian side.

For a couple of dollars, he was smuggled to the border; everything went well until he came across the frozen river. The minute his group stepped on the Russian side, all the people were rounded up and brought to jail. It was his luck that my friend was on duty that day.

Siolek stayed with us until April 1940, when he decided to go back to his hometown to recover some of the jewelry he'd left behind.

CHAPTER 7

TO SIBERIA

On June 5, 1940, a Saturday morning, we woke up to the sound of screaming and crying. The Russian NKVD (the secret police, named for the Russian "Narodnyi Komissariat Vnutrennikh Del") and the militia had started to round up all the refugees from their homes. The people were loaded onto trucks and transferred to specially prepared cattle cars. Each car had a built-in wood stove and toilet, ready for the long trip to Siberia.

All those who were registered as refugees were loaded into trucks with their pots, pans, bedding, and furniture. Children, pregnant women, the sick and the dying, young and old, all were sent to places they'd never heard of before. For the time being, they were the unhappiest people in the world.

Little did they know that the Russians were saving their lives. After the war, whole families came back alive with their children and grandchildren, while most of those who stayed home were killed by the Nazis.

Sure, they had it tough working in the camps, restricted in their movements, and living in the wilds of East Asia, but compared to us, they lived in the Garden of Eden. It was better to live through that than to live in ghettos, be put in concentration camps, and see the smoke rise from the chimneys of the crematoria. Who could imagine in 1940 that only a year later, the devil and all hell would be back again. In the meantime, we were getting ready to live under the Russian communist regime. In the beginning, everything was wonderful. They were our liberators: no more discrimination, no more poor and rich. Everybody was equal; 90 percent of the workers were employed by the government. Many of the businessmen—many of whom had lost their stores—organized cooperatives to get working papers. Tailor cooperatives had one or two real tailors, and the rest just sat around. The same was happening in other trades.

The candidates from the Communist Party won by 99 percent in the 1939 election. Political parties no longer existed. The Russians paid special attention to the young people. They opened youth clubs all over town for meetings and dances, free schools, and free doctors and hospitals.

Life was returning to normal. My father's grocery store was permitted to sell merchandise the government stores did not have. The shelves in their stores were always empty. They sold a pound of sugar or flour once in a while, but most of the time, they sold things that nobody needed. So we were selling everything at so-called gray-market prices. That meant that we paid high taxes and were permitted to buy food from the farmers or any other places we could find. The taxes amounted to twenty thousand rubles a year, but they rushed the payments so it only took ten months to pay up. The last two months, another six thousand rubles were added. Our father would say, "I'm willing to pay as much as they want, as long as I don't have to work for them."

The year 1939 passed, and 1940 wasn't much different. Papa had the store, and Beniek (my younger brother) worked in the bakery. My sister Frieda went to school, and I was working at the railroad.

Because of Father's social status, we were now second-class citizens. The Russians put many restrictions on us; for instance, we could not join the Komsomol (the Russian communist youth organization). On our passports was written, "Jewish, supported by a businessman." It was better to be the child of a thief or a prostitute. In those cases, only the parents were guilty. The children had all the privileges of a Soviet citizen.

CHAPTER 8

LIFE IN STALIN'S PARADISE

My work at the railroad consisted of removing the axles and wheels from the cars and replacing them with wider ones. The Russian rails were a foot wider than their European counterparts. In order to be able to get out as many goods as possible from Poland, the tracks and cars had to be widened. The work was very hard. After removing the axles and wheels, we had to load them onto flatcars and send them to factories for reconditioning. The working conditions were not the best. We had no union to represent us, or a grievance committee to listen to our complaints. The boss was the government, and we did what we were told. The supervisors were all Russians, each of whom wanted to show that he was more important than the others. The result was a different order every five minutes. Not much work got done.

The only reason for sick leave was a temperature of 39 degrees Celsius (102 degrees Fahrenheit), and then only with the company doctor's permission. Your private doctor did not mean a thing. Once, while working outside in very bad weather, I did catch a cold, and I was out of work for two days. A letter from my doctor did not help, so I was fired from my job.

It was still better than what happened to my brother a few months later. He was working at that time delivering bread, and I worked at our father's store. I took his place at work one day. I knew the manager, who saw me sign in and didn't say anything. I worked the whole day, brought the bread wagon back, and said goodbye to him. Two weeks later, my brother received a letter saying that he must appear in court to face charges of laziness. If you left your job to look for another, you were called a butterfly—someone who flew from job to job. Everyone had to appear in court for sentencing. All this happened in 1940, after comrade Malenkov made a speech in the Kremlin about the conditions in the factories. "We want quality, not quantity," he said. "Our products are so bad that more than fifty percent are rejects, and even the items that do pass are no good. We will cut the wings of the butterflies." We all had a workbook and could change our jobs only when we were permitted or released by our workplaces. Well, my brother went to court. He was fined three months at half pay for missing one day of work.

Now, the courts were something to write about. Most of the cases heard in our town were for crossing the border or coming into our city without a special pass, or for refugees who were not sent away or did not leave the city. If a wife or husband were living in Zasanie before the war but one of them was not from there, then they both had to move away, or else the non-resident went to jail. People said at the time, "God gives life, and the prosecutor gives years." Twelve Ukrainians got a total of two hundred years for crossing the border.

I spent many Saturdays in court, listening to court hearings, since they were more interesting than the movies. Most of the pictures were about life in a *kolchoz* (collective farm), or the adventures of a *stachanovets* (work hero) in a factory, where the hero always gets the girl. Older pictures showed the Russian Revolution. No crime or detective stories, no criminals. In the communist Garden of Eden, the public prosecutor once said, "We don't have thieves in Russia. Before the war in capitalistic Poland, the poor had to steal from the rich. But now everybody is poor, and what can one poor man steal from another?" It turned out that the prosecutor wasn't poor after all: somebody later broke into his apartment and cleaned out a few fur coats that he'd confiscated from the rich.

The court consisted of a judge, a prosecutor, and three jurors. The jurors were picked from among the factory workers. The defense lawyer could not put up much of a defense, so most of the accused were sentenced to prison.

The court was in the center of town on Miczkiewicza, and the prison was a few miles away, in Czarneckiego. Let's say ten prisoners had to be moved from court to prison. They were lined up in rows of two. Then two policemen with bayonets on their rifles marched in front—two in the back, and two on each side. The prisoners were led through the city streets, and if one prisoner managed to escape, then the policemen grabbed the first person they saw. As long as they had ten prisoners, it didn't matter to them who it was.

My father had an encounter with Russian law in January 1941. We sent two sleds to Lviv to get some merchandise for the store. On the way back, the militia stopped one of the sleds and brought it to police headquarters. The sled had two barrels of oil, five sacks of flour, and two sacks each of sugar and salt. The militia picked up Father and took him to the office of the DA, where he was interrogated and let go. They confiscated the merchandise. This happened on Friday. My father's friend worked in an office; he took out the proper papers, and we never heard about it again.

We were also plagued by the fear of informers. Anybody could be one: your best friend, or a member of your immediate family. You were afraid to talk in your own home. You were also afraid to talk in front of your children, because they were asked in school to tell what their parents talked about. Many people wound up in jail as a result of not being careful about what they said in front of their children. A saying at the time was, "Watch out—somebody's listening. Who? Either me or you."

We also had to watch how we spent our money. If you went to a nightclub, you had to be careful what you ordered to drink. Vodka was OK, because it was a working man's drink, but champagne was a no-no. A friend of mine made that mistake and ordered a bottle of champagne. He left the bottle on top of the table instead of hiding it underneath. The inevitable happened. The NKVD came and asked him who'd paid for the bottle and then took him away. We never saw him or his family again. We heard they were sent to Siberia. The NKVD went to his home and found some hidden liquor, because his family had owned a liquor store before the war.

There were three kinds of citizens in the USSR: "those who have been in jail, those who are in jail, and those who will be in jail." On the entrance to the NKVD was a sign that read: "Khto nye byluh toy budiet, khto bylh nye zabudiet." ("Anybody who wasn't here, will be; anyone who was will never forget.")

There was always the fear of Siberia. Every once in a while, rumors started to spread that all the businessmen would be sent away. Lists were being made up of all the undesirables, including my family. After the war was over, I was sorry that they did not send us away. The whole family would have been alive instead of only me.

The war was progressing in Europe by this time. In April 1940, Germany invaded Denmark and Norway. In May, it was Belgium, Luxembourg, and Holland. Germany even invaded France. The supposedly powerful Maginot Line didn't stop the Germans; they just went around it.

I remember a movie I saw in 1939, before the war started. It showed how powerful our ally France was. To the west was the sea, the south the mountains, to the north was Belgium (an ally), and to the east was the Maginot Line. It was really *magnifique!* It was impossible to imagine anybody strong enough to break through the deep bunkers, heavy guns, and the underground rooms for miles and miles. Nobody did. They just bypassed it.

The French army did the same as the Polish army: they ran. On June 14, 1940, Paris was taken.

Everybody knows the story of the Dunkirk fiasco. On June 10, Italy declared war on France and England, and on June 22, France surrendered. In October, Italy invaded Greece. On November 20, Hungary joined the Axis, Romania on November 23. It looked like the Germans were taking over Europe country by country.

This was the second winter of the Blitzkrieg. I was working with my father in the store by day and cleaning the snow off the railroad tracks by night. This was how the year 1940 ended.

In January 1941, something new was happening. Big trucks loaded with mixed cement were rushing through the city streets toward the river. Day and night, the trucks went back and forth. There was no stopping them. Nobody was permitted to approach them. It took a whole month to find out what was going on. They were building bunkers, and that meant war. The bunkers went deep underground, with just little black mounds showing up top. Those were thick layers of rubber over the top of the bunkers so that the bombs would bounce off.

On April 6, Germany invaded Yugoslavia and Greece. Japan and the USSR signed a non-aggression pact. On April 17, Yugoslavia surrendered.

We had a partial mobilization. "It is only a test," we were told. All my friends had to register for the army. I, too, had to go. This was the second time. In 1939, I'd come before the Polish medical board but was rejected—flat feet.

The Russian army did not reject me. Out of two thousand men who'd come with me, only two were found to be unfit. On the evening before we were sent home from training, the commander said in his farewell speech, "Now you are members of the glorious Red Army. Aren't you happy to be able to become heroes of the Soviet Union?" He stood the two rejects on a table. Pointing at them, he said, "Isn't it better to be healthy and be able to defend our country than to be in their condition?" Those two were really in bad shape. One was a hunchback, and the other was almost blind. The Polish army did not take men with glasses, flat feet, or other minor defects, but the Russians didn't care: as long as you could walk and stand up, you were good for the army. When I told the doctor that I had flat feet, he said, "Nitsevo, tankistom boodiesh." ("Don't worry—we'll give you a tank to drive so you don't have to walk.")

In May, many older boys were called into the army. It looked like a major mobilization was underway. We lived near a public bath (*banya*), which was taken over by the army, because it had so many men that the military facilities were insufficient. It was necessary to use the public banyas from ten in the morning until way past midnight. The soldiers stood in line to take baths; there was no way for the civilians to get in. Very few apartments had baths in those days, so it was really bad in the cleanliness department.

Smugglers came across the river from the German side with saccharin and flints for cigarette lighters for our store. They told us that the German *Wehrmacht* (Nazi Germany's combination army, air force, and navy) was bringing in a lot of war materiel and soldiers were very close to the border.

The tension was building again—just like in 1939. We, the people without workbooks, had work again. It was May, so there was no snow. This time the job was much bigger: digging anti-tank trenches. All the work was done with shovels and elbow grease. The trenches were five feet deep, their walls reinforced with railroad ties.

CHAPTER 9

HERE WE GO AGAIN! (SECOND BATTLE FOR PRZEMYSL)

June 21 was a sunny, warm day. It was Saturday, and everybody was out in the zamek, the castle park I mentioned earlier. We spent the evening in a pavilion drinking beer and dancing and didn't come home until two in the morning. We didn't sleep much that night. A little after four, we heard an explosion. Then another, and then a whole series of them. It stopped after half an hour, and we went back to sleep. Papa said, "It must be another ammunition dump like the one that blew up a few weeks ago." Nobody knew if it had been an accident or sabotage.

At five o'clock, it started again. This time there was no letup. Now we saw flashes nearby as well as fires. The Germans were pouring artillery shells into the city. Some of the houses along the river were already on fire, and many people were killed. Everybody was running around, not knowing what was happening. The Russian guns were silent. The soldiers didn't know what was happening. It must be war! The Nazis were ceaselessly hitting the city. Still, no answer from our side.

People were in a real dilemma: Should they go to work or not? We had nobody to call for information. The fear of being called lazy was so implanted in people that they did not care about the shooting and headed for work. Many of them were killed on the way. My brother came back a few hours later. Nobody had shown up at work. That was the last time he worked for the Russians. By ten that morning, the Russians started to fire back. It took them that long to get orders from Moscow. The attack had come as a surprise. They had kept their side of the deal in the non-aggression pact they'd signed with Hitler. The Russians were delivering food to the Germans by the trainload. A lot of it was passing via our railroad bridge, the only one left over the river after 1939. When the shooting started, the Germans stopped a twenty-car transport of wheat in the middle of the span. They attacked the train and killed the crew.

After the war, I heard a Russian song about this day that went something like this: "On the twenty-second of June, exactly at four o'clock, they bombed Kiev and notified us that the war had started." I still can't understand why it took Moscow such a long time to order the army to shoot back. The first artillery fire started from our side from the hills surrounding town. No Russian soldiers remained in the city. They had all run away.

At twelve noon, we were all gathered in the cellar. The house was shaking on its foundation from the explosions, but now it became quiet. It was the calm before the storm. The screams coming from upstairs let us know that the devil had come back to finish the dirty work he'd started in 1939. "Alle raus! Schnell, schnell!" (Everybody out! Hurry, hurry). They came into the cellar and chased everybody out. We rushed up into our apartment and grabbed some bedding, clothing, and anything else we could lay our hands on and ran out into the street.

The picture we saw was hard to believe. German soldiers with machine guns at the ready were chasing people from the buildings into the streets and hitting them indiscriminately with rifle butts. Every once in a while, we heard a volley from a machine gun, and that made us run faster. Older people were falling down, while others stepped over them. The Germans were pushing us toward the bridge, where they could take us across. My family—my father and mother, my sister and brother, and my cousin

Saul and I—tried to stay together when a command "Stehen bleiben!" stopped us in our tracks. "Alle zurueck!" (Go back). We started to run in the opposite direction. We were separated but met up later by our home. By that time, the Russians were lobbing shells into our part of town, so we had to get away.

One of our customers, Mrs. Plesniak, whose husband worked for the city waterworks, lived on top of the water tower located on Szczytowa (Summit) Street. The city waterworks were located in the valley near the river; the water was pumped up to the tower and then piped down into the city. Four deep chambers were sunk into one of the highest hills. Two had pumps, and the other two were water chambers from which the water flowed into town. It took us two hours to get there, dodging the exploding shells and hiding in doorways to avoid the German patrols.

It became quiet in the evening. We ate supper and then went to sleep. We awoke to the sound of a loud explosion in the yard. Grabbing our clothes, we ran toward the tower, cannon shells bursting all around us. In the darkness, we reached the tower and started descending the spiral metal stairwell: about sixty steps around a steel pole. Sliding and slipping, we finally reached bottom. The sounds inside were very weird. The *thump, thump* of the pumps sounded like the heartbeat of a giant monster. We were sitting on big pipes, and every exploding shell on the outside sounded hundredfold inside the echo chamber. That's what it was. Fifty to sixty feet deep, with thick cement walls, and empty and cold. When the fighting stopped for a while, Mr. Plesniak, Father, and I went up into the house to get some blankets, warm clothing, and food. Nobody knew how long we would have to sit down there. When we came up, we discovered why the German fire had been directed at us. The Russians had set up an observation post directly on top, and their cannons were below us. It went on all night long without a stop, slowing down for a while and then starting up again. We could hear the shells whistling when they flew over us or burst right next to us.

On Monday morning, the Russians stopped shooting; by eight, it had become silent except for the pumps. After a while, we decided to go up. No soldiers were around. They'd just vanished. When we came out, we saw a picture of total devastation. The beautiful garden of yesterday had changed into a battlefield. Broken trees were all over the place. Vegetables and flowers were pulled from the ground as if a herd of elephants had passed through. The windows in our house were broken, and dust and broken dishes were all over the floor. It took us until late in the afternoon to clean up the mess.

During the day, we could see Russian soldiers advancing down into town, where street fights were in progress. The Red Army was fighting the Wehrmacht, trying to take back the city. And take it back they did. The sound of machine-gun fire and the explosions of hand grenades could be heard all day long. At night, no sound came from downtown. The city changed hands. The Germans were still there but were no longer fighting. They were lying in the streets, doorways, and store windows. They were all dead—killed when the Russians took back the city.

We left the Plesniaks on Tuesday morning, with the idea of returning home. We started walking down the hill together. A sudden burst of artillery fire made us run in all directions, and we became separated.

I found myself in a hospital separated from my family, and I couldn't be released for the whole day. The bombardment did not let up until late in the evening. I was scared and worried about my family, since I didn't know what had happened to them. The hospital was overcrowded with the sick and wounded, and many people had run in from the street to avoid being killed. The nurses tried to chase us out, because they lacked both food and space. On Wednesday morning, the hospital guards forced out all the non-sick people into the street. It was quiet. I started to walk down the steep Wladycze Street until I came to the bottom of the hill on the corner of Franciskanska. The street was strewn with the bodies of dead German soldiers. I found a few people hiding in a basement, so I stayed with them.

The Russians left town on Sunday but returned on Monday morning, when heavy street fighting ensued. Almost all the German soldiers were killed where they stood. I saw bodies in doorways, in store windows, and in the street.

The Russian soldiers took all the men and boys out from the buildings and ordered them to pick up the bodies and throw them into the ditches we'd dug in the school yard as a protection from the air raids. The bodies started to decompose and they smelled very bad, but we were only too happy to be able to bury dead Germans.

Thursday was the first day we could leave the cellar, and I was able to run to our apartment. Nobody was there, but I was told that my family was hiding in a building on Franciskanska. It is hard to describe the happiness in their faces when they saw me. They were sure that I'd been killed and couldn't believe that I was alive. The shelling from the German side kept increasing, and we were forced to leave our building because our house was only two blocks from the river. The whole family moved a few blocks away, where it was safer.

On Friday morning, June 27, the Russians informed us that they were going to leave because the Germans had broken through and threatened to encircle the town. Knowing what awaited us at the hands of the Nazis, we didn't hesitate. We packed up the few things we could carry and headed east.

CHAPTER 10

THE FLIGHT EAST

The roads were packed with Russian trucks and tanks, but civilians were not permitted on them. Every once in a while, an empty military truck came back to pick up stragglers and injured soldiers. Despite those efforts, many of the soldiers were left behind and later died in German POW camps.

We were at a main intersection that was under extremely heavy artillery bombardment. The bodies of people intermingled with the carcasses of horses, burning tanks, and all kinds of vehicles brought up visions of *Dante's Inferno*. The terrible smell of decomposing bodies in the July heat and the swarms of flies forced us to run. The stench followed us for miles. After a few hours of brisk walking, the sound of explosions finally faded. Tired, hungry, and thirsty, we walked into a farm, only to be chased away by the Ukrainian owner. He came at us with a pitchfork, yelling, "Go away, you lousy Jews! I am not going to waste good food on people who'll be killed as soon as the Germans get here." We ran away. We found an empty barn and ate the food we had in our packs, and that was how we spent our first *erev Shabbat* (Friday eve) as refugees.

On Saturday morning, rested but hungry, we started to look for food. The only edible things we could find were green apples from the trees and cold water from a well. Father decided that we would stop in Dobromil, where he had a good friend, so we started out on our way. It was a very hot day, and I drank gallons of water. I could hear the water sloshing around in my stomach as we walked. I spent a lot of time at the side of the road.

We could hear loud explosions around noon, and we came to the conclusion that the Germans had outrun us and that we were now behind the front. We still pushed on and saw the reason for the blasts. The retreating Russians were destroying the fuel and ammunition dumps. Gasoline barrels were flying in the air, setting the wheat fields on fire. It looked like fireworks on the Fourth of July.

It was late in the afternoon when we arrived in Dobromil. The town was in an uproar. The streets were filled with people. The last Russian soldiers were leaving, and the Ukrainians were waiting impatiently for the arrival of the German army. The houses were being decorated with swastikas, and bands of thugs were roaming the streets and beating up Jews. We arrived at the house of Papa's business associate, where we intended to rest for a day.

Sunday was a day of waiting. The Russians left, but the Germans had not moved in yet. We were afraid to leave the house. The streets were patrolled by self-proclaimed militias, which consisted of Ukrainians wearing red armbands with black swastikas. In the afternoon, large signs with greetings for the German army started to appear on the walls around the city. We lost all hope in being able to outrun the Germans and decided to stay there and wait for whatever might come our way. Cousin Siolek, brother Beniek, and I went to another house for the night. Mother, Father, and sister Frieda stayed in our friend's home.

Early Sunday morning, the German army marched into Dobromil, and the nightmare started all over again, as if you were forced to watch a horror movie over and over. The Ukrainians took over the town and spread a reign of terror directed against the Jews. They blamed the Jews for everything that had happened to them during the Russian occupation. Only the women dared to go out, to buy food. Any Jewish male caught in the street was beaten and arrested. On

Monday morning, we were again in the hands of the devil. The Ukrainians kept their promise. They were running from house to house, chasing out the Jewish men and forcing them to clean the streets. Elderly bearded Jews, wearing tallisim and hitched to wagons like horses, had to pick up horse manure with their bare hands.

Around noon, Papa was taken from the house to work; when he did not return at night, we were sure we'd lost him. Our mother was crying all night, but in the morning, our father came back. Just as in 1939, he was probably the only one to return. He was beyond recognition. His hair had turned gray, his clothes were torn, and the smell of decomposed bodies made us choke. We had to bury all his clothes. After he showered, he told us what had happened to him.

He had been in the backyard when the militia took him, along with two hundred other Jews. They were taken to salt holes in the area, where they were forced to remove the bodies of political prisoners shot by the retreating Russians. These were deep holes in the ground that were used in the production of salt. Dobromil had water wells that contained large amounts of salt. Tree branches were laid over the holes, and saltwater was poured over them. After the water evaporated, the remaining salt was collected and sold as kosher crystal salt. They had to work until all the bodies were removed. They slept in an open field; during the night, Father gave one of the guards some money and was permitted to escape.

After this incident, we decided to return to Przemysl. Dressed in farmers' clothing, the whole family started for home. We were afraid to stop anywhere, so we marched without resting until we'd made it back to Przemysl. A Jewish man with a horse and wagon whom we'd met on the road gave my mother and sister a ride. We expected them to be home before us, but to our dismay, they weren't there when we got back. There was nothing we could do but wait and worry. They showed up late in the evening, tired and scared. They told us that a farmer had stopped them and forced them to take the body of a dead Jew, whom he had probably killed. They had to stop at the cemetery, where they buried the man.

Our apartment was a mess, the windows and dishes still broken and strewn all over the floor. It took a couple of days to put everything in order. We were thankful that the store had not been broken into, thanks to its steel door. Most of the other stores had been emptied by the roaming mobs.

We had to get used to life under the Nazis. The walls of the city were covered with official *Bekanntmachungs* (announcements) concerning Jews. Every Jew had to wear a white armband with a blue Star of

David on the right arm. Noncompliance was punishable by death. Every day, new anti-Jewish laws were decreed, and everything was punishable by death. Jews were caught in the streets and taken to forced-labor camps, from which many never came back. Schools were closed for Jewish children, and our food rations were cut in half.

CHAPTER 11

LIFE UNDER THE NAZIS

The Germans set up a *Judenrat* (Jewish council of elders), which assumed responsibility for all matters that affected the Jews in our city. Even converts, or people whose grandparents were Jewish, were now forced into the Jewish community. In the meantime, Jews were seized in the streets and dragged off to perform forced labor, where they were beaten and very often killed and buried in mass graves.

A man named Dr. Duldig, who was a good friend of my father's—they knew each other from their days in the Austrian army—became the first president of the Judenrat. He was a German Jew who had attended school with the German commandant of our town. He used his influence with the German commandant by making a deal in which the Judenrat would deliver Jewish workers to all the necessary jobs, thus preventing the Germans from seizing people in the streets.

Some of the other duties of the Judenrat included the registration of all Jews, tax collection, and the issuance and collection of payment for ration cards. An *Arbeitsamt* (work exchange) was established, and every Jew ten years or older had to register for work. People with money could get a letter from a doctor stating that they could work only while sitting down. There weren't very many of those kinds of jobs, so they were generally excused from doing hard work.

I worked for a while for the Wehrmacht at different jobs and then as a street sweeper. In the beginning, everybody made fun of my street-sweeping job, but people later paid money to get it. The Jews were forbidden to be in the streets from ten in the morning until five in the evening. The only Jews permitted to be in the street were the street sweepers like me, the Jewish police, and people with special permits. Any infraction of this rule was punishable by death. By being in the street, I had a chance to buy food from the farmers. The city dump was located on the outskirts of town, and we could get the farmers before they came into the city. I could buy milk, butter, or eggs and try to get it home. Doing so was *verboten* (forbidden), but everything was verboten for the Jews, and everybody tried to stay alive.

Just throwing a cigarette butt on the sidewalk or not removing one's hat for a German soldier could land a Jew in prison, and from there the next stop was the cemetery.

As time passed, the Judenrat became the instrument of the German authorities, doing all the bidding of the masters. All the terrible blows the Nazis prepared for the Jews came from the Judenrat.

The winter of 1941/42 brought real hardship to the Jews of Przemysl. There was little enough fuel for the other townspeople, but for the Jews, there was almost nothing. Farmers were forbidden to sell any wood to the Jews, and the prices on the black market became very high.

The food situation was even worse. The food rations were minimal, and most of the people did not have any money. Everybody had to work, but nobody got paid for it. The Judenrat opened a public kitchen for the poor, and the majority of us were poor.

The Germans impressed on the Jewish population their doctrine of collective accountability. For the crime of one, many had to pay; as usual, the Jews suffered the most. The German propaganda against the Jews did not let up. They tried to stir up hatred toward Jews. Most of the Poles and Ukrainians were only too happy to oblige. The Jew was portrayed as a filthy, lousy, diseased rat that had to be isolated or the whole population would be infected.

Japan attacked Pearl Harbor on the seventh of December 1941; the United States declared war on Japan the following day. On the eleventh of that month, Germany and Italy declared war on the United States. Our hopes that the war would not last much longer began to soar. The news from the eastern front was bad. The German army was moving into Russia and was meeting little resistance from the Red Army.

In January, the Germans ordered the Jews to give every piece of fur in their possession to the German army, which was busy fighting in Russia and destroying the communists. We had to give up children's fur earmuffs, collars, mink, and sealskin and all our expensive fur coats. The best furs were sent to Germany; the remainder went to the front. As a sign of protest, people did not cover the places where the fur had been removed—like the collars—and wore their coats in the street. The Germans gave an order to cover these bald spots. Anybody who disobeyed was sent to prison.

Once a month, the Germans emptied the prisons—not by freeing the prisoners but by taking them to the cemetery and shooting them. It did not matter why a Jew was in prison; if a Jew was in prison, then he (or she) was as good as dead.

Once in a while, we had surprise visits from the *Hitlerjugend*. Young kids, ten or twelve years old, roamed the Jewish neighborhoods, throwing stones at store windows and mercilessly beating up old people.

In April 1942, the Germans demanded that the Judenrat deliver one thousand men to be sent to a labor camp. Lists of mostly young people were made up; one night, the German, Polish, Ukrainian, and Jewish police went into Jewish homes and dragged out all those who were on the lists. If somebody on the list wasn't home, then they took away any man they found in the home. A few who didn't move fast enough were shot in front of their families. Cousin Siolek, who lived with us, was taken away.

The men were taken to the prison to be counted and registered, which took the whole night. The police kept running through the street and bringing in people until they'd filled the quota. In the afternoon, the one thousand men were in prison, getting ready to be transported. As usual, money played a big part in saving those who could afford to pay. By paying off the police, a few prisoners were let out; others were taken from the streets in their place.

After two days, they were all loaded into cattle cars at the railroad station on Czarnieckiego Street. At some point during the night, the train left for the Janowska camp in Lviv, a hundred kilometers from our town. As I mentioned before, my cousin Siolek, my close friend Nusiek Birken, my father's old friend

Mr. Kupfer, and many other friends were sent away on that day. We had no news about them for a while—only rumors—but after a couple of months, some of them managed to escape and return home.

I would like to relate the story Nusiek told me after he escaped and subsequently returned home.

He said, "We heard a banging on our door about eleven o'clock at night, when we were already asleep. When we opened the door, a German soldier joined by a Jewish policeman and a Polish policeman piled in and in a loud voice called out my name. When I answered, I was told to get dressed, pack a few pieces of clothing, and come with them. My crying mother held on to me but was brutally pulled away by the German. A group of friends stood out in the street, surrounded by police, with their families crying and begging the Germans to let their children go. They were chased away, and the prisoners were marched off to the prison on Kopernika Street. The prison was filled to the brim with people. There was no room in the cells, so we were kept in the corridors, where we stood all night and all day.

"The Judenrat sent in lunch and dinner, and we stayed there overnight. During the day, many of the prisoners were taken out, and others were brought in. They told us that they had been grabbed in the street by policemen and taken to the prison. We found out that for money, the policemen were releasing prisoners and replacing them with people they'd grabbed in the streets. This was going on all day.

"Early in the morning, we were taken to the railroad siding on Czarnieckiego and loaded into cattle wagons. They shoved in about eighty people into a space adequate for six horses. It took a lot of pushing and whipping before they were able to close the door. After some shuffling back and forth, we started on our journey. Our destination was the Janowska camp in Lviv, a hundred kilometers from Przemysl. It could have been a thousand because of what we went through at that camp. I was sure that nobody would get out alive.

"The camp was a labor camp, but it was geared for the destruction of its inmates. Everything had to be done in *Lauf tempo* [on the run]. All day we heard the scream, 'Schnellmachen, verfluchte Juden!' You had to wash on the run. Run for your morning coffee, and you had to be careful, because it could be your last one.

"The camp commandant had his morning fun by standing on the balcony of his home inside the camp and shooting at the inmates. Some mornings his aim was good, and he was satisfied with killing one or two, but if he missed and injured a few people, then the SS men took the injured and finished them off. Being sick meant death. We got no medical help.

No slave since the beginning of history has worked under such conditions. In the first six months, about three thousand prisoners died, through malnutrition, overwork, liquidation, and many other ways only the sadistic German mind could conceive of. I was there from May until July 1942; when the camp was liquidated, I managed to escape and make my way home."

Our hopes for a quick end after the United States entered the war turned to dust. The German war machine seemed as invincible as its propaganda claimed it to be. We could find no news to brighten our hopeless, helpless lives. We listened to the BBC, though it was verboten for a Jew to listen to the radio. We had our own news agency, the *YVA* (for *Yidn Wiln Azoy*, or *The Jews Wish It That Way*), and even that news agency couldn't find any good news. Japan was winning in the Pacific; in June, the Germans took Tobruk in Africa.

Rumors started to circulate that the Germans were planning to open a ghetto, which meant that no matter how bad it was at the present, worse things were in store for us in the future. While we still lived among the Christians, the Germans were holding back on the special treatment they had planned for us. Not that the Poles or Ukrainians cared what was done to the Jews. Quite to the contrary: they were happy about our misfortune. It was the outside world that the Germans were concerned about. On the inside, behind the walls of the ghetto, nobody could see what was being done to us. I was still a street cleaner, my brother Beniek worked for the Wehrmacht, and Papa had the grocery, now a food-distribution store for the Jews.

Once the ghetto rumor became a reality, plans were developed to leave some of the Jews on the outside. For one thousand US dollars, it was possible to get a permit to live in the city, near the ghetto. Father was interested, but lucky for us, he decided at the last minute not to do it. The Germans played another trick on the Jews. They designated a five-story building on Mnisza Street as an extension to the ghetto, and the people moved in; as soon as the ghetto was opened, those people were given twenty-four hours to move out. Not only was their money not returned to them, but they had to leave behind all their possessions.

CHAPTER 12

THE FIRST *AKTION*—THE GHETTO

While I was sweeping the streets, I could hear the gentiles remarking, "Przed wojna, to byly nasze ulice, a wasze kamnienice, teraz sa wasze ulice a nasze kamnienice." ("Before the war, the streets belonged to us and the houses belonged to the Jews; now the houses are ours, and the streets belong to them.") Now the streets were also being taken away from us. The twenty thousand Jews were going to be pushed into an area populated by four thousand people.

One day, Dr. Duldig, the Judenrat president, announced that he would be able to facilitate the ghetto edict if we would give the Germans thousands of dollars. We gave silver, gold, and jewelry, and when we told him that we had no more, he said, "A Jew is like a lemon. Every time you squeeze it, you get out some more juice, and even when the lemon looks dry, give it one more squeeze—a few more drops will always drip out." All the money we gave to Dr. Duldig did not help, and in June 1942 the ghetto was established. Announcements in German, Polish, and Yiddish were pasted all over town.

The ghetto was to be located in a congested slum area of the city. On one side, the ghetto bordered the river, and on the other the railroad track; the other two sides had a barbed-wire fence. The Targowica (the farmers' marketplace I mentioned earlier) was located inside the ghetto territory. To make it possible for non-Jews to reach it, a barbed-wire fence was built in the middle of the street so that one sidewalk belonged to the ghetto, but the road and the other sidewalk were outside the ghetto. It was forbidden to deal with the farmers over the fence. Anybody caught would be immediately shot. That was just to start. As a matter of fact, everything was verboten for the Jew.

Eventually, the dreaded day of the big move came. In one week, all the Jews had to leave their homes and move to the ghetto. It is impossible to describe the shocking scenes that took place in the streets during that week. Everywhere was wild panic and terror. People ran all over town looking for any mode of transportation so that they could

move their belongings. Long rows of makeshift vehicles were heaped with household items. Crying
children, the old, the sick, and the half-dead, all
moved toward the ghetto. Along the curbs stood
the gentiles (non-Jews), joking and laughing. Our
family moved ahead of time. Dr. Duldig—who, as
I mentioned, was a good friend of my father's—arranged an exchange of our apartment and store
with a Christian who owned a store in the ghetto.
Papa got a horse and wagon, and we moved all
the merchandise from our store and the furniture
from our home to the new location. The store,
with an apartment in the back, was located on the
Targowica, right on the boundary of the ghetto.
The sidewalk next to the store was in the ghetto,
and a barbed-wire fence was only two feet away. I
spent long hours sitting on the steps of our store
looking at the non-Jews on the other side. I was very
envious of the young boys and girls who passed by.
They were free and without a worry, and here I was
sitting with the knowledge that something terrible
was going to happen to all of us in the ghetto. It was
very hard to get used to our new location. I wasn't
used to living in one room that served as a kitchen,
bedroom, and living room. We were still better off
than many of the others. Because of the shortage
of apartments, two and sometimes three families
occupied one room. The ghetto also had a shortage

of sanitary utilities, so an epidemic of typhoid fever started to ravage the ghetto.

We thought the ghetto already had too many people, but the Germans thought otherwise. They brought in a few thousand Jews from the surrounding villages. People were sleeping in hallways, basements, and anywhere that had a roof.

Despite the terrible conditions, some Jews felt secure, because nobody was permitted into the ghetto. In the city, meanwhile, roving bands of German criminals entered Jewish homes and took whatever they wanted.

On the fifteenth of July, the ghetto was closed. We didn't know at that time what plans the Germans had for us, but we were sure that their intentions weren't good. One week after the ghetto was closed, rumors started to circulate that an *Aktion* was coming. (An Aktion was a mass operation in which the Nazis assembled, deported, and murdered Jews.) People started to look for jobs with the Wehrmacht as well as with the construction service and other German workplaces in order to secure their *Arbeitscheins* (work papers); others worked for the Judenrat. Because there were more applicants than jobs, you needed "vitamin P" (protection) or lots of money to secure a work permit.

Father and I had the papers, because we had the food-distribution store for the Judenrat. My brother

Beniek was picked up with other workers for his job with the Wehrmacht every morning and was brought back every evening to the ghetto.

On June 24, 1942, the Gestapo notified the Judenrat that they would start the Aktion on the twenty-seventh. The Judenrat was ordered to collect all the work papers and bring them to the Gestapo for validation. About that time, around twenty-two thousand Jews lived in the ghetto. About seventeen thousand lived in Przemysl at the time the Germans occupied our town, and five thousand were brought in from the surrounding small towns. We were waiting impatiently for the return of Dr. Duldig.

Since early in the morning of the twenty-sixth, thousands of anxious people waited in front of the Judenrat for their stamped work papers. When Dr. Duldig returned, he had only five thousand of them, which meant that seventeen thousand people would be sent away from the ghetto. Terrible fights broke out when people found out that their papers weren't being given back to them.

We were also affected. Father brought back only my stamped work permit; his was not returned to him, which meant that I was the only one who would stay behind. At that time, I was laid up with typhus and was unable to get out of bed. I am unable to describe the shrieks coming from all the apartments, including our own. All our relatives and friends assembled in our apartment with bundles of clothing, ready to leave early in the morning. We were told that this was an resettlement and that the people would be sent to villages in the east that had Jewish government, police, money, and post offices. They would work there for the Germans, because the Germans needed workers to take the place of the soldiers fighting the communists. We were so gullible that we believed them. People went to the transport dressed in their finest clothes.

Mr. Kupfer, whom I mentioned earlier, came to our apartment with his wife and two daughters. They were going to leave together with my family in the morning. During the night, Mr. Kupfer died of a heart attack. His family cried all night. Mother sat near me and assured me that one day she would be back. It was still dark, and we could hear screams and the sounds of machine-gun fire outside.

CHAPTER 13

DAS UMSIEDLUNG (RESETTLEMENT)

My father and mother, my twelve-year-old sister, and all the others (my brother Beniek slept where he worked at the Wehrmacht) took their bundles and left for the reshipment center. I suddenly found myself in an empty apartment. A deadly silence enveloped me after all the lamentation during that terrible night. Well, I wasn't alone. On the sofa at the foot of my bed lay the dead body of Mr. Kupfer.

I don't remember what went through my mind. I was in a daze and fell asleep, only to be awakened by a thunderous banging on the door. I woke up with a start when the door was pulled open. An SS man was standing with a machine gun in his hand.

I closed my eyes, and I could feel in my mind the bullets ripping through my body. He asked me why I was in bed. After the shock passed, I realized that he was talking to me. I showed him my stamped paper and told him that I had a bad cold and could not go to work. He asked me where my family was, and I told the SS man that they'd left for the transport. Looking at the other bed, he wanted to know what the man was doing, so I told him that he was dead. He pulled out his bayonet and poked it into the straw mattress to make sure that nobody was hiding there. He looked around the apartment and walked out without another word. I was stunned, unable to believe that I'd come out of that ordeal alive.

I am not sure, but I think that I had another visit from a SS man at some point, or maybe it was a dream. In the afternoon, I felt somebody shaking my shoulder. A Jewish policeman came in and could not believe that the SS man had left me alive. He gave me some water and promised to send help. People came in that evening and removed Mr. Kupfer's body. My temperature shot up, and my body was bathed in sweat. A nurse came and gave me some aspirin, and I fell asleep.

In the morning, machine-gun fire again woke me up. The Aktion continued. Lucky for me, my temperature went down, so I washed myself and put on clean pajamas. I hoped that I wouldn't be bothered again, but no such luck. I had another visit from another SS man the following day. As if in a bad dream, I went through the same interrogation, and it seemed as if somebody were watching over me. I started to tremble after the SS man left, unable to believe that I'd made it two days in a row.

Some of my friends came to my house, loaded me on a small wagon, and decided to take me to the Jewish hospital, which was located in the city. They brought me to the ghetto gate, but I was not permitted to leave. My friends had to take me back home. Here again fate intervened. On the third day of the first Aktion, the Gestapo and the SS went to the Jewish hospital, took out the very sick, and shot them. The hospital personnel and any patients who were able to walk were taken to the reshipment center and sent away with the transport.

I received good news in the afternoon: my father had not been sent away with the transport. A group of men, including my father, was selected to work for the Gestapoman Reisner, who was in the rag business and needed twenty men to pick rags. The group was placed in jail until the Aktion was over, which lasted a whole week. The last transport left on the third of August, 1942.

CHAPTER 14

FATHER'S RETURN

I have no way to describe the hugging and tears when Papa came home. I am sure he was asking himself the same question I had: "Why did we survive when all the others were gone?" We also received postcards from those who'd left with the transport. They wrote that they'd arrived at a village, but they didn't write where. The people in the ghetto felt relieved.

In the meantime, my temperature subsided, and I started to feel better. Father was working in the city collecting rags and was able to bring home some milk and butter. He also hired a woman to take care of me.

During the week of the Aktion, five hundred men, women, and children were sent away. Those who hid were permitted to come out from hiding and were given permits with oval stamps. I suppose the Germans knew that the Jews weren't going to run away and that they would get them the next time.

We got very bad news about the transport. One of the railroad men came to the ghetto and told an unbelievable story. The train went to the Belzec camp. All the railroad men had to get off the train, and an SS crew took over. A few hours later, the empty train was given back to them. We found out later that the postcards with printed messages were given to some of the people on the train. They were forced to sign their names, and address the postcards to their families. Unbelievable rumors started to circulate that the Germans were shipping people to gas chambers and crematoria. Not many believed that civilized people like the Germans would do such things.

The last day of the Aktion, I was told, was the worst. In the beginning, the people went to the reshipment center in large numbers, but as the days passed and they saw how the Germans were treating people, the numbers dwindled. People were hiding in cellars and attics. The SS men went on a rampage, killing those they found in hiding and grabbing anybody they found in the street, even those with work papers.

After the Aktion, the Gestapo demanded that the Jews pay for the trains that were used in transporting the people to the camp. We also had to pay for the barbed wire used in putting up a new fence around the smaller ghetto. They also arrested all the converts, and despite their promises to the Polish bishop, the converts were taken to the Jewish cemetery, where they were shot and buried in a mass grave. Dr. Duldig and his family also disappeared during the Aktion. The rumor was that the commandant of the city had saved them, but later on we found out that the Gestapo had shot them all. Little by little, life was returning to normal—as normal as could be in the ghetto. People had to look for places to live, because the ghetto was reduced to half its size. We were lucky that we didn't have to look for a new place.

I heard a story that the Wehrmacht and the Gestapo were ready to fight over a few Jews, some of whom (such as my brother Beniek) worked for the Wehrmacht. The soldiers picked up the workers every morning at the gate and brought them back to the ghetto in the evening. On the first day of the Aktion, the Gestapo would not allow the workers to board the army trucks, because they did not have stamped work permits. The military commandant closed all the bridges and stopped the Gestapo from moving the trains with the Jews from the ghetto. Only after the Gestapo received an order from the governor of Kraków did they let the workers leave; from that day on, the workers stayed at their workplaces. We saw Beniek only once during the second Aktion.

One day we had a real scare. Father and I were eating lunch when we heard a knock on the door. When I opened it, there stood a *Schupo* (German policeman) in the doorway. When he saw the fear in our faces, he said, "Haben Sie keinem Angst" ("Don't be afraid") and handed us a letter from my cousin Siolek. We hadn't heard from him since his departure for the Janowska labor camp. Siolek wrote that he'd become friendly with a German who was going to help him escape. Siolek was a watchmaker by trade, and now he repaired watches for the German soldiers. In the meantime, Siolek asked for money and clothing. The policeman told us that for two $20 gold pieces, he would be able to arrange for papers and get Siolek back to Przemysl. After a couple of weeks, the Schupo came again, and my father gave him the money. We waited impatiently for Siolek's return but were very disappointed when the German came back without Siolek. He told us that Siolek had been released from the Janowska camp for the weekends, which he was spending in a nearby village with Jewish families. The German had made out an arrest warrant for Siolek with an order to bring him back to Przemysl for an investigation, but when he came for my cousin, all the Jews from that village had been sent away, and he could not find out where. He showed us the papers, and that was the end of that. We never got our money back.

I remember a time when Siolek had come to us in 1939. It was two weeks after the Russian army had taken over our town. He came from Rzeszow, which was occupied by the Germans at the time. His family had immigrated to Palestine shortly before the war, and he was left to liquidate their jewelry store, as I mentioned earlier. The Russians caught him along with many others while crossing the river, which was the border between Germany and Russia.

A friend who was a prison guard came to me and told me that a guy by the name of Siolek Rubin claimed to be my cousin. My friend was able to get him out, but the others were sent to Siberia. Siolek lived with us until he was sent to the Janowska camp.

My health improved by this point, and I had to find a job. Through Father's connections, I landed a job as a watchman in the newly established *Stadtische Werkstatten* (city workshops), where all the possessions left by the deported Jews were cleaned and repaired, to be shipped to Germany. Six hundred people worked there.

The shops were located in the armory, which was a three-story building on Czarnieckiego Street with lots of large rooms. The Germans brought in all kinds of machinery they'd confiscated from the Jews. Production was in full swing in a very short time. The tailor shop repaired all the clothes that had been cleaned in the *Washerei* (laundry). After they finished with all the clothing, somebody came up with the idea of making ladies' suits that used prayer shawls as decoration on the bottoms of the skirts and jackets. A prayer shawl is an oblong piece of white cloth made of wool with black stripes running along two sides, with fringes at the four corners. They were a big hit with the wives of the Gestapo men. The shoemakers, in addition to repairing shoes, also utilized the leather straps from the *tefillin* (phylacteries) to make sandals; the assistant manager, Mr. Teich, thought of that idea. Phylacteries are small leather boxes that contain four handwritten sections of the Torah, to which leather straps are attached; traditionally, men and boys over thirteen place these on the head and left arm during daily morning prayers. Now they were used for sandals. Electric appliances, sewing machines, and items of furniture were repaired and shipped to Germany. Nothing was wasted.

CHAPTER 15

THE SECOND *AKTION*

B ecause the Jews in the ghetto knew what had happened to the people from the first Aktion in July, many of them decided to build bunkers where they could hide if another Aktion should occur. The backyards started to fill up with earth they'd dug up from under the houses. Others built secret rooms and brought in supplies of water and food. They were determined not to go like the others.

On the sixteenth of November, a German police-man whom we called Der Onkel (uncle) came to the ghetto—he'd bought gold and diamonds from a few of the Jews for a long time—and put down an order for a couple of thousand dollars' worth of jewelry. He gave them the money in advance and told them that he would need the merchandise in a few days. When rumors started to circulate that the Germans were getting ready for another Aktion, people said that it could not be true. They pointed out that Der Onkel had left a lot of money with the Jews, and he would know if something were going to happen. Only two days later, on the early morning of the eighteenth of November, it happened.

On that day at five o'clock in the morning, while I was on duty in the shops, somebody came in and told me that the ghetto had been surrounded by SS troops. I could see from a window that Ukrainian, Lithuanian, and German SS men bearing heavy weapons now surrounded the ghetto, as if they were going into battle against the Russians.

All those who worked were ordered to assemble in the shops on Czarnieckiego Street, and after 8:00 a.m., nobody was permitted to leave. The Gestapo and their helpers went into the Jewish apartments and drove everybody out to the reshipment center. I could see through the window how the Germans were chasing the children, the old, and the sick, most of whom could hardly walk. With whips and canes, they beat the people and made them run. A wet snow was falling, and people were slipping, but the enraged SS men were hitting them even more. Some of the people were shot where they fell.

I was worried that Papa was among those who'd been caught, but I had no way of finding out what had happened to him. I heard that some of the workers who'd gone to the gate on their way to work had been apprehended and taken to the transport. The train was loaded in the afternoon, and this time I was able to witness the terrible behavior of the SS men. The screams never stopped for a second. It did not matter if it was a woman or child; people were beaten ruthlessly and forced to climb into the cattle cars.

The Germans were unable to fill the quota of eight thousand Jews they were expected to send away. People were hiding in bunkers, under roofs, and in cellars. Only thirty-five hundred were sent away. The Gestapo came into the shops and ordered all the people out into the yard for a roll call. When everyone was assembled, they read the names of those who were permitted to stay; the others were taken to the reshipment center. The name of my friend Heniek was called, but his wife's was not. She was holding on to her husband, and when a Gestapo man pulled him away, she threw herself at the German's feet, pleading to let him go. He said no and kicked her, but she held on. It took a few minutes until Dawidowicz, who was the head manager of the shops, came over and managed to get Heniek back.

We heard about many heartbreaking scenes after the selection. A son came back to the shops, only to find his father gone from the cellar where he'd been hiding. A mother came back to find the place where her child had been hidden empty, and nothing could be done to help them. The Germans searched the whole building from the roof to the basement and took everybody away. They, too, were sent to the reshipment center. Before the end of the Aktion, the Germans liquidated the orphanage and took away the eighty children who'd been left without parents after the first resettlement.

An estimated forty-five hundred non-working Jews were left in the ghetto by this time. Two days after the Aktion, the Gestapo decided to make a ghetto for those who'd managed to stay hidden in the bunkers. The Jews didn't trust the Germans' promises, though, and refused to come out. Only after the trustworthy members of the Judenrat had gone around assuring the people that it was all right to come out did the Jews leave their bunkers. The Gestapo permitted the workers to return to their apartments to retrieve their possessions.

The SS left the ghetto at twelve noon exactly; only the Gestapo men now walked around. The gates between the two ghettos were opened, and we were permitted to go to our homes. I went to our apartment and found the door smashed and the furniture in splinters. We lived on the ground floor, and the Germans had broken through to the cellar in their search for Jews. I found nobody alive there, which meant that my father had been with the transport. I started to cry for my loss, looked around the room, and walked out into the yard, ready to go back to the shops. "Now I am alone," I said to myself.

I didn't know what had happened to Beniek. I was wandering around the backyard when a neighbor came over and told me that my father was alive and hiding in a building the Germans used to store furniture. For the moment I was stupefied by the news, but after a few minutes, I ran into the building and started to call his name at the top of my lungs. After a while, I heard movement behind a pile of furniture. I ran over and pulled away broken armoires, and then I saw my father. I could hardly recognize him. He was still a good-looking young man of only forty-three, but the happenings of the last few months had aged him a lot. Being hidden by himself with all the screaming and shooting going on around him and the memory of what had happened to him just a few months before showed in his face.

We embraced after a few moments of silence, and tears of relief flowed from our eyes. We realized that I had a big problem. How would I get Father into the shops? Where would he live in the future?

Officially, no Jews were left in ghetto, except those who worked in the shops and for the Wehrmacht. We went to our apartment to get some clothes, and then we returned to the shops. Czarnieckiego Street was crowded with people who were carrying all their possessions in bundles on their backs. Many more people were returning to ghetto A than were coming out. (I'll get to ghettos A and B momentarily.) I saw a man carrying a sack on his back in which something was wiggling. I asked him what he was carrying, and he told me that it was his young son.

The Gestapo men were standing around, quietly smiling. They probably thought, "You Jews think you outsmarted us, but we'll get you next time. You aren't going anywhere!"

We came back to the shops, and I looked for a hiding place. None of us believed that the Gestapo would forgive those who had not reported to the transport and allow them to stay in the ghetto.

As I mentioned before, the shops were located in an armory, which had a small blacksmith shed and a small space under the floor that was used as a drain for horse urine. That space had enough room for Father to lie down, and I put the cover over him. I threw straw on top, and Father spent three days there. It is hard to describe the condition he was in. He aged during that second Aktion to the point that he now looked sixty. We then had another surprise. All those who worked for the Wehrmacht came back, Beniek among them. He stayed in the ghetto for a couple of days, and then went back to his job at the

Wehrmacht. We moved in with three other families who lived in a three-room apartment.

We didn't trust the Germans and waited for the next Aktion. We hoped that Germany would lose the war. The news from the fronts was good. In October, the British army started the offensive at El Alamein. In November the Allies landed in North Africa. After that, the British retook Tobruk, and the Russians began their counteroffensive near Stalingrad.

The job of cleaning out the ghetto then started. Every day, groups of workers went into the empty homes, removed everything that wasn't nailed down, and brought it back to the shop for processing. In many instances, they found relatives or friends who had been shot or died from gas that the Germans dropped into their hiding places. Many of the bodies were decomposed or half-eaten by the rats.

A few weeks later, we heard that the ghetto would be enlarged. Not as large as it had been before the Aktion, but it would have more room than it did now. It would consist of ghetto A, for the workers, and ghetto B, for all the other Jews. In the meantime, about six thousand Jews lived in what was to be ghetto A, which had room for two thousand people. It is hard to imagine living in those conditions. People were sleeping in hallways and in cellars.

It was getting colder now. Winter starts early in our neck of the woods, and we had shortages of food and fuel. The fifty-bed hospital was closed, and all the patients were shot during the Aktion; the doctors and nurses were sent away. A public kitchen was opened, where long lines of people stood in the streets waiting for a bowl of soup. There was no work to be done, and many people were shot while trying to smuggle in food from the outside.

CHAPTER 16

GHETTOS A AND B

When all the apartments were cleaned out, the Germans told the Judenrat that the ghetto would be extended to Kopernika Street and that the people would be permitted to return to their apartments. We now had two ghettos, as I mentioned earlier: ghetto A for eight hundred workers, and a very small ghetto B for the four thousand who'd managed to hide out during the second Aktion. Until the beginning of February 1943, there was no official separation between ghetto A and B. With the arrival of SS Sturmbannführer (Major) Schwamberger, however, ghetto A became a labor camp, and we could no longer move freely between the two ghettos.

Schwamberger came to Przemysl after he'd liquidated a camp in Rozwadow. He brought with him a few of his Jews: Jonas, Wasserman, and a few others, plus our own Teich and Dawidowicz, whom I mentioned earlier (from the workshop), who were ready to help him manage the camp.

The two ghettos were separated by Rokitnianska Street, two barbed-wire fences, and two gates.

The Judenrat started to function again, in ghetto B now, with Dr. Kronberg as president. A man named Mr. Leidner and my father became partners in a food-distribution store, where people could buy food for coupons given out by the Judenrat. It wasn't much, but it helped. I lived in ghetto A, and my father moved into a one-family house with four other families. Beniek still lived and worked with the Wehrmacht.

The winter of 1942/43 was a hard one. It was very cold, and there was no wood for heating. People used unnecessary pieces of furniture for firewood in the beginning; then, as time passed, they used anything that would burn to feed the fire. All the trees and wooden fences disappeared, then the doors and floors went. Somehow we believed that we'd make it. There were no radios in the ghetto, but we did have a news agency (as I mentioned) called *YVA*, and their news was very encouraging. Every once in a while, somebody brought news from the eastern front. In February the name of Stalingrad sparked new hope in our wretched lives. It was hard to believe that the invincible German army had been defeated. We hoped that this was the beginning of the end of the thousand-year Reich. The mighty German army that had marched all the way to Stalingrad had been destroyed, and the ninety thousand who had survived were now being marched, ragged and hungry, into POW camps in Siberia.

We, too, saw a little bit of their Stalingrad trouble. Though we were far from the front, we could perceive what was happening. Very often, the Germans took our people to unload trains arriving from the east that were filled with masses of frozen bodies, many without hands, legs, noses, or ears. The carpenters in our shops were also busy making caskets for the German army. Our people were happy and willing to work day and night at this kind of work. Our hopes were very high that it would not last much longer and that we would somehow make it.

I remember a joke that was told in the ghetto at the time. A Jew wanted to commit suicide, so he took poison, but it was *ersatz* (substitute) and nothing happened. Then he tried a rope, but it broke because it was made of paper. "Well," he thought, "if I slap a German soldier, he'll surely shoot me." So he walked over to a soldier and slapped him. "Now I'm finished," he thought, but the soldier lifted his hand and said, "Was ist lose? Ist der Krieg beended?" ("What's happening? Is the war over?") People believed in the mediums and Ouija boards that were predicting the war would end shortly.

My job as a watchman in the barracks wasn't that bad. I felt pretty good now, and I forgot all about my sickness. The only problem was that I had no money. We didn't get any pay. We didn't pay rent, and the soup was free, but we had no money to buy other things. Then somebody came up with an idea.

The laundry had a few rooms loaded with new clothing the Germans had robbed from the Jews that was now ready to be shipped to Germany. The problem was that the rooms were always locked and sealed for the night. Our original plan was to climb in through a window that a boy who worked there would leave open for us, but we had to give up that idea, because the windows were checked every evening. Opening the lock was fairly easy, although removing the seals the Germans used gave us a hard time for a while; we eventually overcame that difficulty and got in.

The rooms were a gold mine. We felt that we were doing a good deed by stealing back the Jews' possessions from the Germans. After a while, though, we had to stop for fear of being discovered, and our source of income dried up.

One day my friend Arale, who worked as a mechanic in the sewing-machine shop, came to me with an idea. He would prepare a few sewing-machine heads, and my friends and I would take them out during the night. Everything was set, so one night my friends Buniu, Eric, and I started to remove the sewing-machine heads. Buniu took one, and when he returned, Eric left. It was after midnight when I put one machine head on my shoulder and made my way home. The streets were empty, and I was walking without fear, when all of a sudden I came face-to-face with Teich and his girlfriend. He was one of the managing *troika*: Dawidowicz, Jonas, and Teich. I froze, and a million thoughts flashed through my head. "What do I do now? How will I be able to escape this predicament?"

Teich came over, looked at the machine, wrote down the registration number, and told me to take it back to the shop. I took it back and told Buniu and Eric to bring back the two sewing machines. I was fearful of what Teich was going to do. I was sitting that night in the office of the *Wasserwerke* (waterworks), which was used as a showroom for the Gestapo wives. The more I thought about my predicament, the more I worried. I started to picture being investigated by Sturmbannführer Schwamberger. I was sure that Mr. Teich, wanting to show how diligent he was, would surely report me to the Germans.

I could picture the beating I was going to get and decided to avoid all the trouble by committing suicide. I found a heavy sash and made a noose, which

I fastened to a lamp hook in the ceiling. As if in a trance, I stepped on a chair and was ready to jump when something stopped me. A thousand thoughts raced through my mind, and I started to feel dizzy. I heard a voice in my head saying: "Don't be stupid! Don't give up so easily. So many Jews have been killed, but you must live. Don't help the Germans kill another Jew."

I removed the noose, stepped down from the chair, and started to cry. I took the sash and cut it up into small pieces, and then my body started to shake. I spent the rest of the night in the shops, afraid to be by myself.

I went home in the morning and told my father the whole story. He assured me that he would straighten everything out with Mr. Teich. Before the war, Mr. Teich had worked at Nussbaum's flour mills, and my father did a lot of business with him. Three sewing machines were missing, according to Mr. Teich, and he wanted them replaced. Somebody else had stolen them, but I had to pay. Two twenty-dollar gold pieces (*chazarlech*) ended the caper, but I lost my job and was transferred to the basement to chop wood for the kitchen. My two partners in crime refused to share the expenses. Buniu claimed that he had no money (which I'm sure was true), and Eric escaped from the ghetto. I never saw either of them again.

I worked very hard but hoped the war would not last much longer. The news was encouraging. In March 1943, the Russians captured Belgorod and attacked the Germans near Smolensk. General Montgomery was pushing the Afrika Korps in Tunisia.

In April, the Russians took Kharkiv, and Montgomery took the last German-held supply port on the Tunisian coast. The news was unbelievable, and hope was visible in everybody's eyes. Then something happened.

CHAPTER 17

THE MAYORKU KREBS AFFAIR

One day on a beautiful evening in May, a man named Mayorku Krebs was out taking a walk with his girlfriend. The Gestapoman Reisner, meanwhile, had also decided to visit a Jewish girl. He went through the barbed-wire fence and came face to face with Mayorku and the girl. Reisner, who was drunk at the time, pulled his gun, but Mayorku, who was a butcher by trade, was faster on the draw. He pulled out his knife and stabbed the German. Reisner fell, and Mayorku, thinking that he'd killed the man, took the gun, sent the girl home, and escaped from the ghetto with two friends.

Meanwhile, the wounded German was taken to the hospital. The news of the incident spread like a wildfire throughout the ghetto. We knew that something horrible was going to happen. Nobody slept that night. The following morning, two boys and I were sent to the power plant to bring a tall ladder to our electricians. On the way back, as we approached the ghetto, we could hear shooting and screaming in the distance. Without thinking, we started to run but were stopped at the gate. We could see a few people trying to hide, while others were being led away by the Gestapo.

When it was over and I got back home, I found out that my father had been caught up in the dragnet. He and Mr. Leidner, as I mentioned earlier, were partners in a store near the Judenrat in which they distributed food for the Jews in ghetto B. They were taken away with the others. A few people were killed and fifty Jews were taken hostage, to be freed only when Mayorku and his 2 friends were delivered to the Gestapo.

The Gestapo as well as the Jewish, Polish, and Ukrainian police searched the city and the neighboring woods for the escapees but could find no trace of them. Days passed, and still there was no sign of them. The hostages were locked up in a jail on Roketnianska, near the ghetto. I was on my way to see Papa when Feingold, a Jewish policeman who delivered food for the prisoners, said he'd take me with him.

Papa was in a crowded cell with twenty-four other Jews. He looked terrible. His unshaven face was drawn, and his eyes were sad. We embraced and started to cry. I said, "Papa, you'll get out of here just as you have so many times before. Those boys will surely be caught—they have no place to go." He looked at me and smiled, saying, "From your mouth to God's ears."

Three days passed, and one of the escapees came to the ghetto for food. He was caught and handed over to the Gestapo. Despite the beatings he received, he did not reveal their hiding place. Again I visited Papa, and he looked very old. The second of the boys came back, and he, too, was apprehended and given up to the Gestapo. Still they could not find out where Mayorku was hiding.

One week passed, and still no sign of Mayorku. One day, somebody threw a stone with a message through a window on Kopernika Street, which was outside the ghetto. It was from Mayorku. He asked that the note be given to his family, who should make up a package of food, money, and a shaving kit. A Christian boy would be back in the evening to pick it up. The note landed in an apartment of a hostage. His wife took the note to the Judenrat, and they notified the Gestapo. The boy was arrested when he came to pick up the package, and he divulged the hiding place.

The Gestapo took three Jewish policemen to the hiding place. Mayorku was hiding under the roof of a house on Reytana Street. The Gestapo told the three Jewish policemen to go up and retrieve Mayorku. The Gestapo man said, "I know he has a gun. He may kill one of you, but the other will get him if he does. If you come back without him, I have a machine gun and will kill all of you."

They went up, and Mayorku was too tired to resist. He was brought to the Gestapo, and we hoped that the hostages would be freed. Two days later, the Gestapo announced that the prisoners were sentenced to death by public hanging.

On the appointed day, all the people were ordered to come to the place where the hangings were to take place. The old, the sick, and the infirm had to be wheeled to the place. The Germans brought their wives and friends to the hanging. A two-story building with a balcony was in the middle of an empty lot. Three ropes were tied to the iron bars on the balcony, and nooses were placed around the necks of the boys. A Jewish policeman was ordered to do the hanging, but he fainted, so another took his place. He kicked out the chairs, one at a time. We had to face the building. The Gestapo was watching us, and anybody caught looking the other way was beaten to a pulp. The last one to go was Mayorku, who with his last breath called out, "Your end is coming! The Germans are losing the war! *Am Yisrael chai!*" ("The people of Israel live!") And then he died. They left the bodies on display the whole day.

The Gestapo went to the prison after the hanging, and I expected to see Papa very soon. Again, the Germans failed to keep their promises. They selected twenty-three hostages to be freed. Mr. Leidner was among them. Papa was left in prison with twenty-six others. I knew the outcome. There wasn't much time to lose. The Gestapo was cleaning out the prison every few weeks, which meant that everybody was taken to the cemetery, shot, and buried in a mass grave.

I believed that this time, too, Father would survive, just as he had so many times before. He had served in the Austrian army in World War I, as I mentioned, and he fought the Russians for two years. He spent a year in Siberia before making his way home. Feingold, who was delivering food for the Jewish prisoners at the time, came up with an idea. Every morning, a prison guard took out an inmate to clean the latrine. It usually took a few hours to finish the job. Feingold proposed that for a few American dollars, he could arrange with a guard to take Father out very early every morning to clean the latrine. Father would be out of the cell for a while, and if the Gestapo should come to get the prisoners, they would miss him; then, after they left, we would be able to get Father out.

I spoke to Father about the plan, and he approved. Once I proposed that we switch places: he should leave with Feingold, and I would take his place. He refused, though, and said to me, "Siolek, I've lived my life, and you are so young—you have your whole life before you. Promise me that you will try to outlive Hitler and keep the family name going."

I gave Feingold a twenty-dollar gold piece, and the guard accepted the deal. Father was taken to clean the latrine at five o'clock every morning. That was the time when the Gestapo came to the prison to take the inmates away. Feingold informed me that the following morning, the Gestapo was scheduled to empty out the prison. I came to the police office to await my father's return. I was very tense, and the time moved slowly. I fell asleep after a few hours but woke up with a start when somebody was shaking my shoulder. I looked up, and when I saw the expression on Feingold's face, I knew that everything was lost and that our plan had not succeeded.

Because of the large number of prisoners, the Gestapo had come at midnight instead of the usual five in the morning, and my father was still in his cell. After so many narrow escapes, his time had run out. I couldn't believe he was gone until a truck loaded with men's clothing came to the shops, and I recognized the blue jacket he'd been wearing when he was arrested. I realized that I was now the only one left alive from the whole family. I lost the will to live, but I remembered the last conversation I'd had with my father and my promise to outlive Hitler. Days ran into weeks and then months, and we were still waiting for the end of the war.

In July 1943, the Allied forces invaded Sicily, and Mussolini was forced to resign and was arrested. Italy opened negotiations for an immediate armistice. Somehow the news reached the people in the ghetto, and everybody was hoping and waiting for our liberation. In August, the Russians retook Kharkiv. Germany was losing on all fronts. Despite the encouraging news, rumors about a new Aktion had started to go around, but nobody believed them.

CHAPTER 18

THE LAST *AKTION*

I n the early hours of the second of September, the ghetto was surrounded by the Gestapo and Latvian SS, and we realized that another Aktion had indeed started. A few people tried to escape from the ghetto; we could hear machine-gun fire, and soon bodies were littering the streets. People in ghetto B were ordered to report to the resettlement place, but the majority hid in the bunkers. The heavily armed Latvians, with the help of German shepherd dogs, dragged the people from their hiding places, chased them to the railroad station, and loaded them into the waiting boxcars. The screams of the soldiers and the barking of the dogs made the people crazy with fear. They were forced to climb into the high boxcars and were beaten when they could not do so. Many were killed in their bunkers by grenades or gas.

On the third of September, the Gestapo came into the shops in ghetto A and ordered all the workers to assemble in the yard for their work papers to be checked. In the meantime, the Gestapo searched the buildings and removed many children and others who were hidden. Parents had to watch while their children were taken away, and many of them ran after them to the transport. Thirty-five hundred Jews were sent away during the two days of that Aktion.

Nobody slept that night. I could hear sobbing coming from all the rooms. Nobody was permitted to leave the shops, so we slept on the floors. On the fourth of September, we were told that we were going to the Szebnie labor camp. A few weeks before the Aktion, we'd heard rumors that our shops would go there. Then, when trucks came to the shops and took away the heavy machinery, we knew that we would soon be shipped out from our ghetto. Only a hundred people were left to clean out the apartments.

Before now, I'd witnessed the loading of the trains from the window of the shops, but this time I was in the middle of it. We were ordered to assemble in the yard and then were taken in groups of twenty across the street, where boxcars were waiting for us. The other transport was for older people and a few children, and the soldiers were rushing them. Everything proceeded in a fairly orderly fashion with our group, although an older man was unable to climb into the boxcar and was beaten by the SS. It took a few hours, but finally we were loaded, eighty to a car. It was very crowded in those cars, which under normal circumstances held eight cows or horses. For Jews, it was the only mode of transportation.

I was happy when I found myself inside the car and no longer had to see the faces of the SS men. It was late in the afternoon when the loading was completed; the doors were locked, and the train started to move into the unknown. For a while it was quiet, but the farther away the train traveled, first the women and then many of the men started to say lamentations and pray. Many of the people, myself among them, fell asleep.

Hours passed, and the sun went down. It was past midnight when the train came to a stop. The doors opened, and the screams of the SS men and the barking of the dogs accompanied us as we jumped down from the boxcars. The train had stopped in the middle of a field, and as soon as the train was unloaded, we were ordered to line up in rows of four and then told to run. Anyone who stumbled and fell was trampled by the others, just as in a cattle stampede. None of us could see where we were going.

The only thought in my mind was, "Get going and don't stop—the dogs are behind you."

The seven kilometers from the station to the camp would fit in *Dante's Inferno*. We made it in no time, hurried along by the screams of the SS and the howling of the dogs. An older woman who had fallen to the ground was kicked by an SS man, and when she couldn't get up, she was hit on the head with a rifle butt. She died, and the rest of us had to carry her body to the camp. I don't know how many of us were killed on that march, but I am sure that all of us were present at the roll call later. We could see the glow of bright lights in the distance after a while, and when we came nearer, I could see a barbed-wire fence, several high sentry towers, and numerous barracks. We had arrived.

We were greeted at the gate by a big sign that read ARBEIT MACHT FREI ("Work sets you free"). We were led to an open space between two barracks. A group of SS officers came over, and one of them told us to hand over all our valuables and money. He warned us that we would be searched and that if they found anything concealed on our bodies, we would be shot on the spot. Ten people were led into a barracks, and when they came out after ten minutes, they told us what had been done to them. They'd had to undress and lie down on tables. Germans in white coats with rubber gloves on their hands examined every inch of their bodies, looking for hidden gold. They didn't find anything, and the people were told to get dressed. A second group was taken away, and people started to dig holes in the ground, where they put their possessions. After the second group came out, we were chased away, and the workers came, dug up the ground, and took out everything the people had hidden there. The smart Jews had once again been outsmarted by the Germans.

I no longer knew what time it was, because they'd taken away our watches. Not much was left of the night when we were led into the barracks and told to go to sleep. We had not eaten since leaving Przemysl, but we were all so tired that we fell asleep, five to a bunk bed.

I was awakened by somebody banging with a stick on the bunk beds and screaming, "Alle raus!" ("Everybody out!") Outside, we were given a slice of black bread and a red bowl with ersatz coffee. We were registered, assigned a barracks, and the men were separated from the women.

I registered as a metalworker and was assigned to a machine-repair shop. It took two days to get settled in, during which time we were left in peace. I was assigned a second-level bunk, and my neighbor turned out to be the cousin of a girl I'd been going out with before the war.

CHAPTER 19

CAMP SZEBNIE

I t was still dark outside when the barracks orderly
started his infernal banging on the bunks. The
scream "Alle raus!" became the morning song during my entire stay in that camp. We were given a
towel and were told to go outside to wash up. Long
water pipes with faucets were spaced every few feet. I
used my finger to brush my teeth, came back to the
barracks, and was given a slice of bread and coffee.

Lined up in rows of four, we were marched to the
Appellplatz (loosely translated as "roll-call place"),
which was a large square in the middle of the camp
in which a mass of people was already assembled. SS
men were on the roofs of the barracks with machine
guns pointed at us. Other SS men with horsewhips
walked among the assembled prisoners. Our names

were called, and it took a long time to determine if everybody was there.

After two hours we heard the command, "Achtung! Stillschweigen!" ("Attention! Quiet!") The camp leader, Commandant Grzymek, marched into the middle of the square and read us the rules of the camp.

"This is a labor camp," he said, "and *Arbeit macht frei*. If you work to our satisfaction, then you will be rewarded with freedom. If somebody breaks the rules, then he will be punished with twenty-five to fifty lashes. When you see a German soldier, you stand at attention and remove your cap. It does not matter where you are or what you are doing. If you are caught with your hands in your pockets, your pockets will be sewn up. Do not attempt to escape, because doing so is punishable by death." He went on like this for a whole hour, telling us of all the crimes that we should not commit. It was noon when they let us go.

Everybody was given a *Strohsack*, a long sack made of paper string that we had to fill with straw from a big mound piled in the middle of the camp. This, too, had to be done *schnell (fast)*. That call, *Schnell! Schnell!* was to stay with us all day long. You had to wake up—*schnell!* You ate and drank—*schnell!* Worked *schnell* and died *schnell*.

We were given a red metal bowl and a spoon and were told not to lose them. This was the only way we'd get our food: no bowl, no food. A ladleful of a gray liquid of some kind, with two or three pieces of potatoes, was all we had for the day. There was no need to wash the dishes. We all licked our bowls and spoons clean.

After lunch, we were given our places to sleep. The orderly gave us a lesson in proper behavior.

We'd all just arrived from homes of some kind; no matter how crowded, they were still our own rooms, with our own families or friends. Now we were among strangers, in a strange place. Five hundred people sleeping in one barracks. The windows and doors were shut, and nobody could leave during the night. Being outside at night meant instant death. And the noises—the snoring, crying, and coughing—meant it was almost impossible to sleep at night, and when you did manage to fall asleep, the orderly would scream, "Alle aufstehen!" and right away his helpers would run along the barracks, hitting the bunks with big sticks. The people would jump down, bewildered, not knowing what to do.

It was five o'clock. It was still dark, and we were lining up in front of the water pipes, with spigots on both sides of us. Everybody was pushing, trying to finish first so they could run back inside to stand in line for breakfast. Next, we stood in the camp square for roll call, surrounded by the SS men holding machine guns. After two hours of repeated counting, we were ordered to go to the shops.

The shops were located in a large barracks, where we saw the machines that had been brought from the ghettos. Our job was to unpack and assemble all the machines. The Germans planned to build an industrial city at this camp, and we were going to work for the glory of the Third Reich. What a future! The Germans also planned to build hundreds of barracks for the new shops.

"Why not end it now?" I thought. " It would be so easy. Just walk over to the barbed-wire fence, a burst of machine-gun fire, and it's all over." But no! Something was holding me back. A voice in my head was telling me, "Hold on—you must keep your promise to your father. You'll make it and will live to see the destruction of your oppressors!"

And so you go on, day in, day out. You get up in the morning, you wash up, you eat your "breakfast," you stand for roll call in the rain—sometimes for hours when the count is not correct. You work, you eat your watery soup, then you work again, six days a week. Sometimes on a Sunday or a Jewish holiday, they give you overtime, like on Yom Kippur 1943.

Instead of going to the synagogue, they had a cleaning job for us to do. All the men and women were put to work moving furniture. There was a big pile of furniture—probably from the nearby ghettos—on an open lot, and we had to move every last piece of it to another lot about two miles away. SS men with horsewhips in their hands stood along the road making everybody run. It took the whole day to clear the lot, and then we had to sweep it clean. We had to move all the furniture back to the old lot the following day, where it was left out in the rain.

I became friendly with two brothers from Rzeszow, the Goldschmidts. After a while, we decided to change our jobs to something outside the camp. It was too dangerous inside, since to many SS men were around. They came into the shop twenty times a day, and every time somebody yelled, "Achtung, Mutzen ab!" ("Attention! Take off your caps!"), we had to drop whatever we were doing and stand at attention until the German said, "Weitermachen!" ("Continue with your work!")

Even in the latrine, we had to do the same thing. We had to get up, let our pants drop to the floor, and remove our caps. We felt very foolish. The Germans laughed as this was funny to them.

We landed a job picking potatoes. Every morning after the roll call, our group lined up in front of the gate and were counted; we then marched out to a farm. There was no stopping. The digging machine traveled up and down the field throwing up the potatoes, and we had to pick them before the digger came around again to cover the potatoes with soil. The soldiers were always watching, and we were whipped if we weren't fast enough. One day at work,

I felt a nail in my boot (I still had a pair of English riding boots at this time) that had pierced my right heel. I wouldn't be able to stop to remove my boot until we returned to the camp. My boot was filled with blood, and I was happy I didn't get an infection. I traded my boots for regular shoes and limped for a while, but I had no other problems with my foot. We had a chance to steal a few potatoes now and then and smuggle them into the camp. Once we had to smuggle a young Jewish boy into the camp. A young boy came over to us and begged us to help him get into the camp. He'd escaped from the Staszow camp two weeks before. He'd been hiding in the woods and eating raw vegetables and potatoes, but now everything had been harvested, and he was hungry and tired. Somehow, we got him in. I don't know if we saved his life or just prolonged it for a short while.

I worked for a while in the repair shop, and then all the work in the shops stopped, and everybody had to work in a large open field adjacent to the camp. Surrounded by guards, we worked rain or shine. We had to pull out sugar beets. It was very hard work pulling those beets. A few people tried to eat them, but they became sick after swallowing a mouthful, since raw sugar beets are generally considered to be inedible.

While we were working outside the camp, two boys managed to escape. The Germans discovered their escape when they were counting us entering the camp. A special roll call was announced, and we were counted again and again, but still two people were missing. After midnight, we were finally permitted to go to sleep. The following morning, the body of one escapee was brought back and placed in the middle of the camp, where it lay the whole day. We never found out what happened to the other boy.

Commandant Grzymek kept a watchful eye on the camp. With a machine gun slung over his shoulder and his finger on the trigger, he was quick to kill. One day the farmers brought in a large amount of straw, which we used to fill the Strohsacks for our bunk beds. The straw was left out in the open, in the middle of the square. The wind was blowing the straw around, and two girls were given the job of sweeping the straw back on the mound. It was a hot day, and one of the girls leaned on her broom to rest, just at the time when Commandant Grzymek walked by. He pulled the trigger without a word, and the girl fell dead to the ground.

Something was always happening in the camp. One day, a boy was beaten by an SS man. The boy yelled out, "Soon the war will end, and then we'll pay you back!" The punishment they subjected the boy to is impossible to describe. He was tied to four stakes in the ground. The sun was beating on him, and the boy had to look into the sun all day long. We were forbidden to give him a drop of water. He was begging for the SS guards to shoot him, but they merely laughed at him. In the evening, he was brought to the camp center and laid naked over a bench, while the whole camp was lined up for the evening roll call. After we were counted, a kapo (a prisoner whom the SS assigned to oversee forced labor) came over with a horsewhip in each hand and started to whip the boy. There were ten thousand people in this camp, and we had to stand and were not permitted to avert our eyes. The boy was sentenced to fifty lashes, and he had to count in a loud voice every lash. His skin had been ripped to shreds by the time he'd counted to fifteen, and then he lost consciousness. The kapo did not stop until the fiftieth lash, but the boy had died long before that.

After the show, Commandant Grzymek told us that we could expect the same treatment if we misbehaved. It was late in the evening when we received our piece of bread and cold ersatz coffee.

It seemed like a lifetime, but we were in Szebnie for only two and a half months. In October, we had a surprise: the one hundred people we'd left behind in the ghetto came to join us. They had an unbelievable story to tell. After our transport had left, the Germans discovered that many Jews were hidden in the bunkers. The Gestapo searched all the buildings in the ghetto, blowing up many of them. They found about three hundred Jews and put them up in two houses surrounded by barbed wire. After that they set up a new Judenrat, with a man named Neubart as president. The Gestapo promised that after a few weeks, all the Jews would be sent to Szebnie. The Gestapo chief gave his word of honor to the Judenrat that all the Jews who would come out from the bunkers would not have to fear any reprisals and would be sent with all the others to the camp to work. The president of the Judenrat went from house to house and repeated this message over a loudspeaker. Because of this promise, nine hundred people left their hiding places. He promised those who were hiding to come out and said that they would be given blue permits, while the others had pink permits. They were housed in two buildings and were told that they would be sent to Szebnie, where the previous transport had been sent. They were told that they would have to pay for travel expenses, because the Gestapo had to order a special train to take them to Szebnie. One day they were marched to a school gym and told to undress for a medical checkup. They were led out behind the building twenty-five at a time and machine-gunned. After all nine hundred people were dead, three men from among the remaining Jews were selected to build a pyre and burn the bodies.

It took over a week to do the job. The sickly sweet smell of burned flesh permeated the air of the whole city; after the job was finished, the ashes were strewn in the fields outside the city. The three men were then taken away and shot.

After the one hundred who were left finished the job of cleaning out the apartments in the ghetto and everything was sent to Germany, they were loaded on a truck and sent to Szebnie. The city of Przemysl was declared *Judenrein* (free of Jews).

One day, a group of men from our camp, including me were loaded onto two trucks to pick up a load of boards for the new barracks. We traveled a couple of hours up a winding mountain road and then down a steep mountain until we came to a lumber mill. The SS men rushed us to load the heavy boards, because they wanted to be back in camp before nightfall.

On the way back, our truck could not make it up the mountain and had to be rolled back into the village. The other truck went back to the camp, and the six of us were locked up in the village jail.

One of the SS men told us to select one man, who should go to the village and arrange to get food. We selected a boy who didn't look Jewish and spoke perfect Polish. Before the boy left, the SS man said to him, "I will let you go by yourself, but you better come back, or your friends will be shot."

We were sitting on pins and needles, wondering if he would return. He did come back after two hours. He was accompanied by a few villagers, who carried a large pot of steaming mashed potatoes and a smaller pot of sour milk. The heavenly aroma of mashed potatoes and fried onions soon filled the jail cell. I will never forget the feeling of happiness we had when we started to eat our meal. I always wondered if the villagers knew that we were Jews, because the boy didn't tell them. After the meal, we went to sleep in the locked jail cell.

In the morning, the villagers brought us some bread and milk. When a replacement truck arrived, we had to transfer the boards and bring them back to the camp.

A group of my friends and I volunteered to go to a new camp. We hoped that we would be able to escape from there. One early morning in late November when it was still dark out, we came out to the roll call and found ourselves surrounded by heavily armed Ukrainian SS men in black uniforms. Some of them were sitting on the roofs of the barracks, pointing heavy machine guns at us. We were counted again and again, and late in the afternoon, the names of those who had registered for the new camp were called out. I was happy to hear some of my friends' names on the list. There were 120 of us.

We were brought into a barracks, and the door was locked. We could not see anything, but we could hear the yelling of the SS men and the cries of prisoners being whipped. It took hours. Finally somebody drilled a hole in one of the boards, and we found out what was happening. It was a selection. Different lists were being read, and groups of people were being led to separate barracks.

We were getting hungry, but the Germans did not send us any food the whole day. Then we saw footlockers at each bunk. That was something we didn't have in our barracks. Some of the more daring among us broke open one locker, and we couldn't believe our eyes. The locker was filled with all kinds of goodies: sugar, butter, dried meat, even wine. In no time, the lockers had been opened and we ate and ate.

The barracks belonged to the sanitation men, whose job was to empty the latrines and deliver the contents to the farmers. While they were outside the camp, they did a little trading. They took out jewelry and money and smuggled in tobacco and all kinds of food.

In the meantime, the others were still standing at the center of the camp. A light snow had started to fall. They were marched out of the camp in the late afternoon, and they remained locked out for the night.

The camp resembled a ghost town in the morning. We wandered around the camp for a while, and the silence was deafening. The guards were manning the watchtowers, and a few SS men remained in the camp, but they left us alone. Later in the day, three trucks loaded with clothing came back to the camp. We were told that the people had had to undress to their underwear and even had to remove their shoes. They were taken to Auschwitz.

We were told to pick out warm clothing and shoes. The trucks came in the afternoon, and we were told that we would be leaving for a new camp.

CHAPTER 20

CAMP PUSTKOW

As I mentioned, I had an eerie feeling of being in a ghost town that last day in Szebnie. Just one day before, thousands of people had been moving around the camp, while today, I could hear a cold wind whistling between the empty barracks. No one was lined up in front of the kitchen, we could eat as much as we wanted, and there was no roll call.

Nobody seemed to be paying any attention to us, and we wandered from barracks to barracks looking for our friends, but they weren't there. All gone. I should have been used to this by now. The three Aktions in the ghetto had had the same effect: a feeling of sadness and a loss of hope. You feel desensitized after a while, but every time it happens again, the whole process repeats itself.

I picked out a warm coat and a pair of good shoes. Much to my surprise, I found two fifty-zloty bills (Poland's currency). This had been a lot of money before the war, but I threw them back. I knew that wherever we were going would have no stores in which to spend it.

Around noon, we were given potato soup with plenty of potatoes and a whole loaf of bread. Three covered trucks arrived, and we left the camp, leaving behind the memories of our dear friends. Two soldiers stood at the back of our truck with their machine guns at the ready. We were told to keep quiet.

I was thinking about the future. What kind of reception awaited us in the new camp? How long would it last, and would I come out alive? So many questions, and who was there to answer them? It took a couple of hours, but eventually we arrived at camp Pustkow. The camp looked new. It had only three barracks, and a few people were already there.

The camp was in the wilderness. We got off the trucks and were lined up in front of a long barracks, and the German camp leader with two nicely dressed camp inmates walked over to our group. One of the inmates introduced himself as the camp leader. His name was Poldi, and his assistant was Strauber.

We stood there for a long time, and then one of our boys asked if he could go to the latrine. They pointed to the end of the long barracks and told us to go, ten at a time. When I came in with my group, I saw a large empty room that was just being constructed. It contained two large wash basins with water faucets all around it. The cement floor had rows of holes in it. We just stood there, wondering what we were supposed to do. After five minutes, a kapo came in and told us to march out. All five hundred of us marched in and out, not knowing what we were supposed to be doing there. Some of the smarter ones found hiding places for their valuables behind the unfinished walls.

When one of the men asked again to go to the latrine, the kapo started to scream, "You stupid jerk, you just came out from the latrine!" When we realized what had just happened, we broke out into loud laughter. They explained to us the purpose of the holes in the cement floor. It took us a while to hit the center of the hole; if we missed, we had to clean the floor. Later on, every time I used that room I had to smile when I remembered that episode.

All our lives were now concentrated around this barracks. At one end were the latrine and washroom, on the other was the hospital, and in the center was the kitchen. It was a perfect arrangement, because if the kitchen gave us bad food, then we had to use either the latrine on one end or the hospital on the other.

We were told to line up, and they took a count. After the roll call, we were marched to the Entlausungplatz (disinfections place). We had to undress, and our clothing was put on racks and pushed into a disinfection room. Our hair was cut, and we went into the showers. When we came out, we were ordered to get dressed. It was impossible to breathe. The SS men were screaming for us to get out. People started to collapse from the fumes emanating from our disinfected clothing. We were chased out from the room and ordered to run. One young boy didn't get up fast enough and was hit over the head with a rifle. We had to carry his lifeless body back to the camp.

Meanwhile, back in the camp, the walls in the washroom were removed, and all our valuables were taken away. The Germans had outsmarted us yet again.

After a medical checkup, we were led to two barracks, with four rooms filled with two-tier bunk beds. There was room for five hundred prisoners.

We were surrounded by a training center of seventy thousand SS men, which was next to a camp of around five thousand Polish prisoners who were taken to the SS camp every day to do all kinds of jobs. The Jews worked inside the camp. All of us were tradesmen: shoemakers, dressmakers, tailors, and woodworkers and metalworkers. We did all our work for the SS men and their wives. They came to the showroom, where they ordered suits and dresses, shoes and gloves, and all kinds of home furnishings.

The shops were separated from our camp by a barbed-wire fence with two entrances: one for us and one for the SS customers. The camp was clean and the food not bad, and the Germans bearable. Only one *Obersturmbanführer* (camp commandant) and three SS men of a lower rank supervised our camp. Every shop had a German headmaster (*Obermeister*) and a foreman. The other SS men could not come into the shops but had to wait in the showroom until one of our men could come out to take their orders.

I worked in the *Schlosserei* (metal shop), where my foreman was a man named Willi Fertig. We became good friends, and he picked me for special jobs. For a while I worked with the Goldschmidt brothers in the blacksmith shop, making railroad spikes. It was much cheaper to do it with our Jewish hands than by machine. We were making hundreds of them, and the overhead was minimal.

The carpenters were very busy. They did not complain, though, because they were making German caskets for the Russian front. They were willing to work twenty-four hours a day doing that, including Sundays.

CHAPTER 21

FIFTH YEAR OF THE BLITZKRIEG

December passed and 1944 arrived. The Blitzkrieg was in its fifth year. The Russians took Kiev and broke the siege of Leningrad. In the evenings, our camp strategists had extended discussions about how long it would take for the Russians to come to us, and if we would still be alive when they got there.

In the meantime, we settled in to our daily routine. Get up at daybreak, run to the washroom (only pants and shoes—no shirt, summer or winter), breakfast, morning roll call, and a short walk to the shops. For lunch we came back to the camp for one hour, during which we could rest or play ball. In the evenings, we had supper and even read paperbacks the Germans gave us. They were all about German heroes, but they were something to read. On Sundays we played ball and did some exercise; in the evenings we put on shows, attended by the German guards and their wives. We had real Viennese actors (prisoners at the camp) and a baritone named Zelazny, who gave excellent concerts. After a while, we started to call the camp "Pustkow Zdroj" (the Pustkow Resort). We wished we could stay there till the end of the war.

The situation in the neighboring Polish camp was much worse. Around the end of April 1944, with the Russian army coming nearer, the Polish prisoners started to escape when they were going to or from work. Those who were caught were brought to their camp, and after being tortured in sight of the entire camp, they were shot and then cremated in a small crematorium the Germans kept handy for small jobs.

The old inmates told us how terrible life used to be in our camp. They told us about one particular SS man who used to detain the last man to leave the barracks and throttle him with a towel. After that, he would announce that the man had hanged himself. They marked it down in the books as a suicide. It was so bad that Jews had started to run away. They got help from a Jewish girl from the nearby town of Krosno whose brother was held in the camp. They were successful for a while, but then an escapee was caught and, after an interrogation, told all. The girl was brought in to the camp, where the punishment was administered by the camp leadership. She was put in a room, and the prisoners were sent in one at a time and forced to rape her until she was dead. Then the brother was hanged.

One night we were awakened by the sound of gunfire coming from the Polish camp, where a mass execution was in progress. About two hundred Polish men and women who'd been arrested in Rzeszow were summarily executed and cremated within an hour.

After a while, the whole Polish camp was being punished. Every time a Pole escaped, the food packages the prisoners had been receiving from home were given to us. Every evening, wagons filled with cakes, breads, butter, sugar, jams, and all kinds of other goodies arrived at our camp. Sometimes we would find money or messages baked into the cakes, which we had to hand over to the SS. We would destroy any incriminating letters or deliver them to the prisoners. It was a lot of fun, because it was always a surprise when we opened a package. We hardly ate the camp food. At that time we didn't know that they were unintentionally saving our lives. We all gained weight and looked almost like normal people. There were no *Muselmänner* (the slang term for prisoners who were so undernourished they could hardly walk) among us.

One day, the SS shop boss brought in two trucks filled with rusty metal parts. He told us that this was "eine Holtzwolle Maschine"—a machine for producing the wood shavings used for packing and for filling the mattresses on our bunks. The machine had probably been built in the 1800s, for the tsar of Russia. That's where it came from. All the way from Russia he brought that museum piece. Two guys from our shop were selected to clean and assemble this behemoth, and I was one of them.

The machine consisted of a large and heavy movable tabletop made of metal with two slits on each end. Steel rollers moved over the slits, and a large shaver and a hundred narrow knives operated in each opening. The roller would press the wood over the knives, and then the shaver would cut narrow ribbons of wood. We polished the knives and tried to figure out how to assemble it. And so passed the months of May and June, and we could hardly believe we would ever make it work.

In July I had to go to the hospital for minor surgery, because my left heel was giving me lots of trouble. I had forgotten about that nail in my boot that had pierced my heel at the Pustkow camp in 1943, but now I'd developed a spur in my heel and could hardly walk. The doctor promised me that it would be a minor operation, so I agreed to do it. I could not stay in the hospital, though, and was assigned to KP duty, peeling potatoes.

On the twentieth of July, I was peeling potatoes when very exciting rumors started to circulate in the camp: something so unbelievable that it sounded like a big lie. Someone had made an attempt on Hitler's life. A bomb exploded in the room where Hitler was holding a briefing, and a lot of generals were killed. We were all excited, full of hope that the war would surely come to an end soon.

All day our excitement went on, and then a big disappointment. A few officers had tried to kill the Führer, but things did not go as planned. A few generals were killed, but Hitler himself escaped with minor injuries. The rest is history; I am relating only what was going on in the little world of our camp.

My foot healed, and I went back to my monster. The machine was ready now, and everybody was waiting to see the finished product.

The opening day was postponed, though, because we had more important jobs to do. Our metal shop was transformed into an armored-truck factory. The Germans brought in open trucks on which the carpenters put up enclosed plywood containers, which we covered with metal plates. We could feel the air of fear. It was showing in the Germans' faces now, and we could hear it in their way of talking.

The Meister of the carpentry shop, called Kune Leml, was a *shmo* (not too smart), even for a German. Every day he brought the carpenters the latest news, but by July the carpenters had to pull the news from him. Once he said, "We may be losing the war, and it's possible that we'll suffer a defeat, but we Germans will go underground and fight until victory is ours."

The crematorium in the Polish camp was very busy. The Germans were bringing in a lot of people from the outside, and we could hear the sound of machine-gun fire at all times of day and night. The Poles were escaping more often now, because they knew the Russian front was coming nearer and that they now had a better chance of making it than they would have earlier in the war. Our people were very anxious that the camp would be liquidated and that we'd all be sent to Germany or Auschwitz.

Our shop got a new supervisor, a young SS man just back from the Russian front. He'd lost his right arm and now took it out on us. For any small infraction, he would beat the offender until blood covered the poor soul. We were looking for a way to get rid of him, until one day he dug his own grave by bringing in an old rusty Russian Nagan for us to clean. The camp leader was notified about the Russian gun, and we never saw the beast again.

At last the time had come to start the wood-shavings machine again. Trucks loaded with wood started to pull up in front of the shop, and we got ready for the grand opening. At the signal, I pushed the starter button, and the giant motor started to whine. I pushed the lever, and the long transmission belt started to flap, turning a wooden wheel near the ceiling. The long shafts and transmission wheels started to whine, pulling a wide belt that ran down to the machine. A silence enveloped the shop when the first shavings fell to the floor. The SS man picked up the shavings with a smile on his face and threw them into the air. We worked for a few hours and filled up a few bags.

One day near the end of July 1944, it was still dark out when the orderly started banging at the bunk beds. Screaming, "Schnell, alle raus!" ("Hurry up, everybody out!"), he chased us out into the street. We were told to wash up, get dressed, and be ready to leave the camp.

At the morning roll call, the camp leader told us that we were moving to another camp, and as proof he pointed to the trucks loaded with all the camp's food, which he said was coming with us. We were put on trucks and brought to the railroad station.

We didn't suspect anything when we were loaded into the cattle cars, because this was the usual mode of transportation for Jews during the war. There were eighty of us to each wagon. That, too, was normal. But when they slammed the doors shut, and we saw the trucks with the food and our camp leader drive away, we realized too late that the Germans had outwitted us again.

CHAPTER 22

DANTE'S INFERNO

Eighty of us were crammed in the darkened box-car. My friends Wilek, Lunek, and I were pushed against the wall of the car. A little sunlight came through the boards covering the little barred window. We had no room to move. We had enough bread and cigarettes to last us, but no water. The heat was getting unbearable, and so was the air. The train stood at the station for a couple of hours, but nobody paid any attention to our pleas for water. Eventually the train started to move again, and we traveled for a few hours. We knocked out the boards and could see the stars. During the night it cooled off inside, and we could breathe at last. I was standing beneath the window and was able to wipe off a few drops of condensed water from the iron bars.

Some of my neighbors were urinating into their hats and drinking it. People were defecating where they stood, and the stench made it impossible to breathe. The train stopped somewhere among the fields, and we tried to sleep standing up, but it was impossible. It was a very long night, and in the morning we started to move again. The sun was starting to heat up the car, and we'd had our last drink of water more than twenty-four hours earlier.

By noon the train pulled into a station. The doors were opened, one car at a time, and pails of water were given to us. It is hard to describe the pushing and fighting that ensued over a few drops of water. The doors were shut again, and we started to move. The water we drank started to turn into sweat, and our car turned into a steam room. If we'd complained about the heat before, this was much worse. The water was pouring out from our bodies, and we were forced to remove our clothing to keep cool.

Some of the older men fainted, and one of them died of heart failure. His son stood by, helplessly imploring us to do something, but there was nothing anybody could do. After the son saw that his father was dead, he went berserk and injured two people with a knife. It took some doing to subdue him and tie him up among that mass of bodies. By now thirst was hitting us again, but there was no more water. We were sure that this would be the end of us. A few of us came to the conclusion that the SS was going to keep us in these cars until we all died of thirst.

The train was surrounded by armed SS men this whole time, and when we started to scream and bang on the doors, they told us to shut up or they would open the doors and kill a few of us.

As the day progressed, with the July sun beating down on the locked cars, the heat became unbearable. The train started to move, and people were fainting from heat exhaustion. The only relief came at night. We were moved to a siding, and we fell into a stupor. We had no water or food during all that time.

The train started to move again the following morning, but only for a short while. Every time a military transport had to pass, our train was pushed to a siding. At noon of the second day, they opened the doors, but they gave only one pail of water to each car. The strong ones started to push, and the others were left without anything to drink. We started to scream, and the soldiers opened the doors and threw pails of water into our faces. The cold wetness felt good for a while, but when the doors were closed again, we started to sweat. It felt like a steam room again. It was hard to breathe, and the older people started to collapse. By now thirst had hit us again, but we had no more water. By now it had become clear to us that this would be the end of us. "They'll drag us around until we've all died of thirst" crossed my mind. Some people started to say prayers for the dying.

I was lucky to be standing under a small barred window, so I was able to collect the droplets of condensation on the iron bars. The train would stop every once in a while; everybody waited for the doors to be opened, but after the military trains passed, we were off again. It was now the third day since we'd started our journey in that hellish train. We received water only once in all that time, and no food at all. The Germans treated their animals better than us.

All of a sudden, the stars I could see through the little window disappeared. The train stopped, and it became pitch-dark inside the car. We were in a tunnel. We could hear the *poof, poof* of the engine. Smoke soon seeped into the car, and people started coughing. The coughing then changed into sounds of asphyxiation. We were sure that the stories we'd heard about how the Germans were gassing the Jews would soon come true for us.

Somebody started to scream, "This is the end! They're going to kill us now! They'll leave us here until we die from smoke inhalation." People started to pound on the doors, while others tried to break through the floor, but they couldn't do it with their bare hands; still others continued to say prayers for the dying.

After half an hour—which felt like a lifetime to us—the train started to move once again. We emerged from the tunnel into a brightly lit area. The train stopped, and we could hear the barking of dogs and the screams of "Schnell, raus, verfluchte Juden!" The doors of the cars were pulled open, and all hell broke loose.

CHAPTER 23

AUSCHWITZ-BIRKENAU

The screams of "verfluchte Juden, schnell raus!" (Damn Jews, hurry up) made us wake up from the daze we'd been under as a result of our extreme thirst. Prisoners in striped uniforms jumped into the cars and started to push us out. Everything was happening so fast that we were taken by surprise. We had no time to get dressed. People fell to the ground and were kicked by the SS men's boots, and the dogs fell over us, scratching and biting. I was pushed out, dressed only in my underwear and one shoe; I could not find the other one. Then we understood what they were yelling. It was in Polish, and it was something I hadn't heard for a while. We'd heard it in Szebnie and in Pustkow, and it was the Germans who'd yelled it at us: "Schnell, verfluchte

Juden!" Now it was the Polish foreman screaming at us: "Parszywe zydy, szybko!" ("Out, lousy Jews!")

He continued, "Leave everything behind—you are in Auschwitz now! Here everything will be given to you!" He also told us not to worry about our clothes. "You will all get uniforms like I have," he said.

We arrived at the place we'd feared the most, the place we'd tried to avoid. We'd landed in hell.

And so we jumped out of the cars and into the blaze of spotlights. For a moment I could not see; my eyes couldn't adjust to the bright lights after three days in the darkness. Then I saw the scenery. We were standing on a wooden platform, and as far as the eye could see were barracks, barbed-wire fences, spotlights, and high sentry towers with the muzzles of machine guns visible through the openings. The searchlights were sweeping the area, hitting our eyes every few minutes.

The first impression was that we were in a very bad place. It took only a second to get accustomed to the view—less time than it takes to tell about it. I was in a daze but woke up very quickly to the screams of the SS: "Schnell, schnell, verfluchte Juden, Schweinenhunde!" And then they let the dogs at us. (I always had an aversion to dogs after this day, even if it were only a Chihuahua; I would get goose bumps just from walking by a dog.)

The dogs started to bark, and the people started to push, trying to get away from them. But there was no place to go. The SS men were all around us, and they held wooden bats that they used on our backs and heads. Eventually, we all stood in front of the cars. The German shepherd dogs were still barking but were kept on their leashes. A group of SS officers came over and checked us out. We were told later that the infamous Dr. Josef Mengele (known as the Angel of Death) had looked us over, and we apparently met with his approval. After the inspection, we were ordered to run. I was limping on my one shoe, while the other bare foot was stepping on sharp stones. We were running now, bewildered by the barking of the dogs, the whistling of the whips, and the screams of the SS men. My mind was a blank. I was just trying to run away from this snake pit.

After a while—a time that seemed to be another lifetime after the endless time we'd spent on the train—we came to a building. We entered a long hallway and were told to undress. We were ordered to spread our legs and lift our arms. After a while, the barbers came and snipped off all our body hair. It was more like pulling than cutting. A few people screamed and were severely whipped by the SS men.

After all my hair was removed from my body, only my eyelashes and eyebrows were left. I was pushed into another room. Before I entered, I first had to step into a basin filled with a green, foul-smelling liquid. A man with a large glove on his hand dipped his hand in the liquid and smeared it all over my body. I bit my lips as I tried not to scream from the pain. My skin started to burn when the disinfectant penetrated the nicks left by the barber.

The room we entered next was tremendous, with showerheads sticking down from the ceiling. Each of us was given a piece of gray, sandy soap. No towels. The sound of locking doors made me jump. Five hundred naked men and boys stood there, looking up at the ceiling, waiting for the water to come from the faucets. And then a terrible thought hit me. I started to tremble. So this is the end. What if the rumors were true? What if gas instead of water comes from the showerheads? And there was not a thing that I or any of these other people could do. Was this the way my mother, sister, and many other members of my family had died? Feeling miserable and deep in thought, I had to jump when a surge of hot water hit my body. A big scream went up around me, it was so unexpected, and we all stood with our mouths open, swallowing the hot water. It was the first time in three days that we'd had a mouthful of that life-giving liquid. Hot water never tasted so good. After a few minutes, the water stopped and we were ordered to soap ourselves. Then a terrible scream rang out as streams of ice-cold water hit our heated bodies like a hammer. The shock is impossible to describe. Despite the surprise, most of us stood with our mouths open, gulping the delectable liquid. Our dehydrated bodies absorbed the wetness.

The doors opened then and we were chased to another empty room. We stood there waiting for towels to dry our bodies, but we received none. Big fans in the windows were used to dry us instead. We hadn't washed off the soap while we were drinking the water, and now our bodies started to itch. People were rubbing themselves against the walls. It looked as if we were doing a ritual dance. It looked very funny, I'm sure, but it was very tragic, and nobody felt like laughing.

The command, "Alle raus!" then made us jump. We came to a long hall filled with tables covered with clothing. Behind them stood skeletons. It was hard to distinguish if these were male or female. After a while I saw that they were girls, because they wore long striped dresses. Their heads were as bald as ours, their bodies flat. We stood there in our birthday suits, but I don't think the girls paid any attention to us. They must have seen such scenes every day. Gray-and-blue striped prison uniforms and shoes with wooden soles were then handed to us. The SS men stood around with horsewhips in their hands, hitting those who weren't fast enough. Tall men put on pants that reached their knees and the sleeves their elbows, short fellows had to roll up their pant legs, and there was no time to exchange clothing. The SS men were watching.

We were told to line up in front of small tables with large letters from A to Z. The order came to roll up our left sleeves, and we were tattooed on the left inner arm. I received the number "A 17996". After all the people had their numbers tattooed on their arms, we were assembled outside. We were told to memorize this number and forget our names. Your name, we were told, no longer exists, and only the number will be used from now on. If we hear this number, we should yell "Jawohl!" (Yes). Otherwise we would be punished. And so Saul Birnbaum ceased to exist and only "A 17996" would now be breathing, eating, and working.

Sometimes I wondered, why I was going on.

Before the war, people committed suicide for many reasons: lost love, bad business ventures, heavy gambling losses, or incurable diseases. We were always ready to throw away our lives. But in the concentration camps, I often wondered why so many of us did not try to do the same. What did I hope for? My family was no more. My name and dignity had been taken away from me. I'd been put into a prison uniform with a yellow marker to let everybody know that I was a Jew. My future was hopeless, and my past eradicated. Even my birth certificate was destroyed, as though I had never existed. This was Hitler's goal, to wipe out an entire race of people.

It would be so simple to end it all. Just run toward the wire fence, and I would be electrocuted or shot by a guard before I could even reach the fence. Or I could refuse to remove my cap the next time I passed an SS man. Why suffer hunger, cold, thirst, and all that degradation? But we had no answers to these questions, only the hope that we would be the chosen ones to see the destruction of the Nazi beast.

Now we had time to look at one another. Despite the terrible situation we found ourselves in, we broke out in laughter. We resembled circus clowns. Our faces were drawn and black from lack of food and water. Three days had passed since we'd had our last meal. The uniforms and the round striped hats looked very funny to us. But there was no time for merriment. The devils were whipping us into lines to listen to the SS officer.

It was already daylight when we walked out to the roll call. We'd spent the whole night getting cleaned and dressed. The camp was coming to life now. People in uniforms just like ours were coming out from the barracks. They had a peculiar way of walking. They didn't pick up their feet; they just dragged them.

It took some time before the prisoners had lined up in double rows; the officer then read us a long list of things that were forbidden, and everything was punishable by twenty-five lashes or death. It was late in the afternoon by the time we were led into a barracks and assigned bunks, five people to a bare bunk. Before we could lie down, though, we got the order to go outside for food: one loaf of black bread and one red bowl filled with hot liquid for five people. We stood there watching one another to make sure that no one would get an extra sip, and when the bowl was empty, we were still thirsty. We were marched to the latrine then and were told that we were allowed to use it only once a day.

Back in the barracks, we lay down on bare boards. We spent the whole night lying on one side, unable to turn. It was a terrible night. We suddenly realized where we were then, and people started to pray and cry. Unable to leave the barracks, people were urinating and defecating wherever they were lying.

In the morning, when the foreman came into the barracks, he started to scream in Polish, "Parszywe Zydy [stinking Jews!], how could you do this?" He made us clean up the place before the SS men came. He launched into a long speech. "My name is Krwawy Janek" (Bloody John), he said. Pointing to a long whip he held in his hand, he said, "I've killed many prisoners with this whip, and when I say jump, you better jump, or you're dead." Then he added, "You see this building with the tall chimney? You walk in through the door and come out through the chimney as a puff of smoke. And this is the only way you'll get out of here."

We stayed in Birkenau (also known as Auschwitz II) for three days. We were permitted into the barracks only in the evening, so we sat outside all day. At lunchtime we received soup and were told by the barracks leader, "Eat this soup—it's made with your parents' fat." A few people started to retch, but when you're hungry, you eat no matter what.

I was observing what the other prisoners were doing outside our compound. Groups of people were working under the supervision of SS men armed with rifles and horsewhips. The whips were raining down on the prisoners' backs. The men were digging ditches, while the women had to carry the dirt on wooden planks to a place across the road. All the prisoners had shaved heads and looked like skeletons; the only difference was that women wore striped sack-like dresses, and the men wore pants and jackets.

After a while, the men were ordered to walk over to the pile of dirt and start loading it back on the planks; the women carried the dirt back to the ditches and threw it in. This went on all day. I surmised that this was another way of killing people.

On the third day, after the roll call and so called "breakfast," we were lined up and ordered to undress.

We stood naked for half an hour, and then a group of German civilians and SS officers came over to check us out. These were the buyers. They came to look over the slaves. That's what it was: a slave market. I'd seen things like this in the movies, and now I was part of it. We had to flex our muscles and open our mouths, and they checked our teeth; we passed with flying colors, except for two men. One was a midget, and the other had contracted jaundice. The buyers purchased us, and we were told that we would leave for work in a day or two.

The thirst still bothered us, so we had to buy water from the permanent inmates by trading bread for water. The water there tasted very bad, since it was muddy; as a matter of fact, the whole camp was built on a pile of mud. As soon as it started to rain, it was impossible to walk. Many people lost their shoes trying to extract their feet from the knee-deep mud. The air had a foul smell of burned flesh about it that never left our nostrils. The chimneys never stopped smoking. This was Birkenau, the death factory where millions of Jews from all over Europe took their last breaths. Their bones were used for fertilizer, their teeth pulled from their mouths to fill the coffers of the Reichsbank with gold.

We were to leave in the morning, and I did not care where, as long as we were leaving this hellish place. Nothing could be worse. And so I slept dreaming of freedom, of how I came home and found that everybody was happy. Germany had been destroyed, the SS were no more, and peace reigned all over the world. The Poles greeted us warmly when we returned to our homes. Everything was given back to us, and the whole family was back together again.

All of a sudden I heard a scream—"Alle Aufstehen, raus verfluchte Juden!"—and the terrible reality came crashing back again. I had to get up and start another day in the hell called Auschwitz. It was still dark out, but as usual the day in camp had begun. We washed up, had our scrumptious breakfasts—consisting of black ersatz coffee and a sixth of a loaf of what they called bread—and were told to get ready for the trip into the unknown.

The trucks pulled up, and we were loaded onto them. We were on our way out, and all the others were envious of our quick departure. We had special luck. While others had spent months before being sent away, and many had left by way of the chimney, we were on our way after only three days in hell.

Soon we were outside the gates, and we left the sign—ARBEIT MACHT FREI—behind us.

CHAPTER 24

GLEIWITZ III

We arrived in our new domicile a few hours later. It was small and did not look like any camp I'd ever visited before. In fact, it was a factory—Die Alte Gleiwitz Hutte was its name—and it was located in Upper Silesia. Gleiwitz was the town where Hitler had staged a phony incident in 1939 that he'd used as a pretext to invade Poland, and thus start World War II. On the eve of the war, a group of Polish soldiers attacked the Gleiwitz radio station. They were really German prisoners, dressed in Polish uniforms and carrying documents of the Polish army. They were all killed and put on display to prove that the Poles were the aggressors.

Our camp was located at the far end of the factory, which was just one large old bombed-out factory building and a smaller one that was used as a garage. We were told that the one newly built brick structure would be our quarters. Oh yes, and I must not forget the latrine. It was the most important place in the camp, as I would soon find out.

We were then brought into our sleeping quarters, which consisted of two large rooms separated by a large dining room; on the end of the building was a small hospital. The building had a basement, in which new toilets and showers were being finished. In the meantime, we had to use the outside latrine and washing facilities.

This was the beginning of August, and we were being moved closer to the interior of Germany; the war was still on. The sixth year of the Blitzkrieg was approaching, and we were still alive.

The entrance to the camp had the standard sign, ARBEIT MACHT FREI, it was surrounded by an electrified barbed-wire, and it had four guard towers, with spotlights and machine guns directed toward the camp.

We lined up for the roll call, and our numbers were called for the first time. We all stood with the sleeves rolled up on our left arms, looking at our tattoos. When a number was called, the owner of that number had to call out in a loud voice, "Jawohl!" Lucky for us, we did not find out what would happen if somebody didn't answer. Later on, prisoners were beaten to a pulp on many occasions for not answering quickly enough. This done, we were then taken to the garage and given wood shavings, Strohsacks, and pillowcases. After we filled them, we were taken to our sleeping quarters.

The room was newly painted, the bunk beds made of new boards, and we were taught how to make our beds the army way. The blankets had to be stretched so tight that a coin would bounce on top. It was easy to accomplish this on the lower bunks, but those who were assigned the upper ones had to be acrobats to achieve that feat. In the beginning it was very hard to do. I had to stand on the sideboard of the lower bunk and, not able to hold on—I had to use both hands to stretch the blanket—I kept falling backward. It took practice, but the fear of missing breakfast eventually made us perfect. After a while it was just like standing on the floor. Each bed was inspected, and we had to do it over again if it wasn't satifactory, which meant that you didn't eat until lunchtime.

After we were settled in, the guards assigned us to our jobs. But first we had to rebuild the factory. We started to knock down the inside walls until a big empty area was left, and then the free workers came in to put up new walls.

I was working in the metal shop. The two Gold-schmidt brothers and I took over the blacksmith shop. Our supervisor was a German civilian who was easy to get along with. We were able to produce cigarette lighters out of brass tubing and old drill bits. Our foreman sold them in the city and brought us bread, tobacco, and other things that weren't available in camp.

After a while, machinery started to come in, so we set up brand-new lathes, shavers, and milling machines. All the shoemakers, tailors, and carpenters were trained to operate the machines. Everything was operated by compressed air, and I was appointed as an operator of a small air compressor. It had only a little bit of air pressure, and it was set up near the blacksmith shop where I worked. I just had to check the safety valve so that the air tank would not blow up from too much pressure.

It was good to work in that shop. It was hot work, but when the cold weather came, it was very pleasant. While others had to work outside in freezing temperatures, we were working in our shirts only. We also baked potatoes. Why did we bake potatoes in a blacksmith shop, you might ask? The answer is very simple. We had a forge, and the fire was always on. We constructed a small metal receptacle under the forge and went into the potato-baking business. And business was good. We had more customers then we could handle. The people working outside hid some potatoes when they unloaded the wagons, and we charged one potato for every four we baked for them. Our only worry was the smell. We were lucky that no SS man came inside the factory, and the civilian workers didn't care as long as we got the work done.

After all the machinery was installed and the air lines hooked up, we discovered that there wasn't enough pressure to operate all the machines. Only some of the machines were able to work, until a new compressor was erected.

CHAPTER 25

DIE RÄDER MÜSSEN ROLLEN FÜR DEN SIEG (THE WHEELS MUST ROLL FOR VICTORY)

We started to dig a five-cubic-meter-deep foundation. It took three weeks to dig, and the job was very hard. The ground was packed with large lumps of molten glass, and the pneumatic drills were unable to break them up. It was a twenty-four-hour job, and I volunteered for the night shift, because no SS men were around to watch. I slept during the day and didn't have to stand in line for chow. Breakfast was left for the night workers.

The German foreman was a civilian who had no love for the SS, so he didn't push us too hard. But sometimes the work was hard. The chisels in the pneumatic hammers often bent and sometimes broke, but we kept on. "Die Räder müssen rollen für den Sieg." ("The wheels must roll for victory.") And so the trains loaded with sand and cement kept coming.

This was October 1944. In July, US forces had broke out of Normandy. In August, Allied troops landed in the South of France, and Romania declared war on Germany, but we kept building a thousand-ton compressor.

In September, Bulgaria declared war on Germany, and Finland signed an armistice with Russia, but we were pouring cement and setting up anchor bolts for the compressor. The bolts were six feet long and had to be carried by two people. Railroad car after railroad car of sand and bags and bags of cement were mixed and poured into the foundation, and all for the glory of the Third Reich.

My shop foreman, Willi Fertig, said, "Let's put Saul on this job, and we can be sure that when the compressor's finished, the Germans will have to blow it up, as happened in Szebnie with the woodshavings machine."

It was work, work, all the time. (Arbeit macht frei!) We were only free on Sundays. That was our rest time, except when a few carloads of potatoes, or a wagonful of cement or iron, arrived. It had to be done right away. The Germans needed the trains to help win the war. So after a six-day work week, we got a little overtime.

Sundays were also devoted to health inspections. We had to undress to the waist and stand outside in all kinds of weather for hours until it was time to go into the doctor's office for the checkup. The camp doctor and his helpers were mostly looking for lice. If they found a louse in someone's clothing, then the owner did not receive his bread portion for two days.

The water pipes froze in the winter, and we had to build a fire to get the water running so that we could wash before breakfast. We had to run out from the barracks and wait to get in line for a faucet. Your upper body had to be bare, and woe to anyone who was caught with a towel over his shoulders. He was beaten mercilessly and could wind up in the HKB. Those were the initials for a prisoner hospital, Häftlingskrankenbau, or prisoner sick bay. We called it Himmel Kommando Birkenau, or Heavenly Commando Birkenau.

Spending even a little time in the hospital meant death. A black ambulance came every once in a while, and all the patients were taken away to the gas chambers in Auschwitz-Birkenau. If somebody was injured while working, then he was accused of sabotage. The SS men were getting paid two marks (or so we were told) a day for each worker. A sick man did not work—no two marks—but they still had to feed the sick prisoner. It was much cheaper to simply ship the sick to Häftlingskrankenbau. Zyklon B (a cyanide-based pesticide) they had in abundance. But food was scarce.

On Sundays, when the SS men left us alone, we spent our time on haircuts and shaves, as well as general cleaning, delousing, and shoe polishing. Our shoe polish was a mixture of burned rags and fine machine oil.

I liked to sit by the window and look out into the free world. Our camp was located on a hill, across a narrow brook from a public park. I could see boys and girls walking and holding hands, and parents and children playing. We could hear music and see people dancing.

What a different world. So near, yet millions of miles away. Laughter and joy out there; tears and despair in here. And always the threat of the crematoria. It was their war, but we had to suffer. Our children, parents, sisters, brothers, and girlfriends either shot or gassed, their ashes thrown to the winds.

In the evenings, while I was working, I would look out into the city and see illuminated windows in the nearby apartment houses. I could see people moving behind them. Free people. People coming back from work, eating supper, and going to bed whenever they wanted, not sleeping in bunk beds, two hundred to a room. Normal humans in a normal world.

Some Sundays, the serenity was disturbed by special jobs. Behind the factory was a stockpile of five-meter-long pipes and very heavy long steel bars. Lying outside as they were, all kinds of dirt and dust got blown between them. Our job was to carry the steel bars and pipes to another location, clean up the debris, and then bring them back and stack them in the same way as before. It did not make sense; it was just harassment. As usual, everything had to be done quickly. The pipes were long, the steel heavy, and by Monday we could hardly move.

Sometimes we had air-raid alarms at night. We had to stop work, while the others had to get up from their beds and run to the basement. It was not a bomb shelter, but they could lock us in and not have to worry that some of us would escape. The camp lights were put out during the alarms, so it otherwise would have been easy to slip away.

One evening during an air-raid alarm, I lost two front teeth. Well, it was not during the alarm but soon after. It happened this way. When the alarm sounded, everybody ran into the supposed bomb shelter. In one corner of the shelter, the bread was being cut for the next morning's breakfast. When the lights came on after the alarm, the guards discovered that many portions of bread were missing. The SS men lined us up and searched everyone, then looked into our mouths. Some of the men would leave part of their bread portions for later. These men now had their bread in their pockets and were accused of stealing. I never saved my bread but instead ate it immediately, but they found crumbs between my teeth, so one SS man hit me repeatedly in the mouth with his elbow. I had to stand at attention while he kept battering away at my mouth. As a result, I lost two upper front teeth. I swear I did not steal that bread; it had been left there from supper. My punishment wasn't the worst: others wound up with bloody heads and black eyes.

Meanwhile, the work on the compressor was progressing. We'd finished the foundation, and the German engineers started to assemble the machine. They predicted it would be ready by January 1945. I had the feeling that the time to be moving again was approaching.

The camp had a grand opening in November. The new washrooms and showers we'd seen when we'd first arrived at the camp were finished and turned over to us. Up until this time, they'd been kept for show only.

It was a pleasure to walk down to the basement and wash in the morning and be able to use warm water instead of ice water. Or to use the showers on Sunday, right in our camp, instead of marching to Gleiwitz I. Twice a month we were marched to the other camp. It was a spectacle. Surrounded by SS guards, we were paraded through the city streets, with people standing on the sidewalks looking at us as if we were a species from another planet. Some of the Germans even asked who we were.

We had a small twelve-year-old boy (a camp mascot, tolerated by the SS men) who was there with his father. When bystanders asked him why he was a prisoner, he answered jokingly, "We are murderers, and I myself have killed five people!" They looked at him, really believing him.

Gleiwitz I had a large building with showers as well as an orchestra, which played marches whenever the prisoners went to or returned from work. We were greeted with music whenever we went there. A few times, famous Jewish actors from Vienna, inmates of camp I, put on a show in our camp. On the evenings when shows were put on, it was hard to believe that we were in a concentration camp. The camp leader and the SS men and their wives sat in the front rows, and the inmates behind them. Most of the shows were in German, then the baritone Zelazny whom I mentioned earlier, a member of our camp, sang opera, and then came joke time. Obersturmbanführer Ruff—our camp leader—told jokes.

The whole camp was tipsy for the first two weeks in December. Some of us were outright drunk. It was much fun, but it ended in a terrible tragedy. Here's what happened. Next to our camp was a Luftwaffe fuel depot, where the Germans kept antifreeze for the airplanes. Our people had worked there for a while, and one day, somebody spilled some of the liquid. Because we were always on the lookout for food, somebody sampled the liquid and discovered that it tasted like liquor. For about a week, people drank themselves to sleep. Our tinsmiths made hip flasks, and a contraband business in liquor started. Those were the happiest two weeks since the war had started. Day after day, the happy juice kept flowing, with no end in sight. We passed those days as if we were in a dream, but the awakening was a shocker.

I myself had had a few sips, and it tasted very good, but then the liquor was gone, and a few boys drank the antifreeze. Nothing was done to save them. They were left outside for all to see. It was a terrible sight. Their bodies were writhed by convulsions, their faces distorted by pain. We could hear their screams all night. And then quiet. Not a sound came from outside. The silence was more nerve-shattering than the screams. When we came out in the morning to wash up, we saw them lying at the side of the building. That put a stop to the drinking.

Just before Christmas, trains filled with new machinery and tools arrived at our camp. It was a whole train with precision tools stolen from Czechoslovakia—carbide drill bits, gauges, and micrometers—all brand-new and still wrapped in oiled paper. Our German Meister made us pack them in oil drums and bury them behind the factory. I often wonder if he ever dug them up, because a fortune was hidden there. We used to trade with the Italian workers at the camp—an expensive micrometer for a few cigarettes or a loaf of bread.

Then, the last bolts were tightened and the last electric wires installed. The owner of the factory came very often to check on our progress. We called him Churchill, and he really looked the part. He was fat and always had a thick cigar in his mouth. Our people always followed him, and fights broke out whenever he threw away a piece of the cigar.

It was snowing when the year 1944 came to an end. We all wondered what the new year would bring for us. The war surely could not last much longer, we thought. For the Christmas holidays, we received pork and mustard—a little pork and lots of mustard—and the boys loved it. Normally we didn't eat pork. But if it came down to eating pork or starving, pork won out. They also gave us German Quargel cheese. This we did not like, but the soldiers loved it. The cheese seeped from the boxes, and the Germans used to scrape it off the boxes and eat it. When we opened the cheese, it stank to high heaven, and white worms were crawling all over the mess. The Germans ate the cheese, worms and all, and were delighted when we gave them our portions.

New Year's Day came and went. The year 1945, was here. How many more years would we be able to take?

The compressor was now ready. The pipes were hooked up, and the machines were ready to start producing artillery shells and help win the war. I wondered how such a monstrosity would be able to turn over, but it started to run on the first try, smooth and quiet. The compressed air flowed to all the places it was needed. It had a few air leaks, but we took care of them quickly. The production of the shells was now in full swing. The civilian workers from the factory took away the shells every evening, and by the following day, a new pile was waiting for them.

It was hard to believe that tailors, carpenters, and shoemakers had been able to operate all that machinery and do a good job. We tested every shell for welding seams, and 99 percent were perfect. A fast course in electric welding, and presto-chango, twenty shoemakers became welders.

Obersturmbannführer Ruff declared the tenth of January to be a holiday. Our people were ordered to sweep the whole camp, because the Germans expected a lot of guests. Higher-rank SS officers and their wives started to arrive around noon, and then the Obersturmbannführer pushed the button and the tremendous machine started to purr like a little kitten. We could hear the air rushing through the pipes and into the machines. Everything was in perfect order. We closed down the compressor for the night; the following morning, I would be in charge of that machine.

In the morning, the German Meister watched me start the compressor. He turned the key, and I pushed the starter button. The machine came to life, and I wondered how many more times we would go through this procedure. Thursday evening was the last time we closed the compressor. My luck held. We never started that compressor again!

The carpenters and metalworkers started to build small pull wagons around the tenth of January. Nobody knew their purpose, but rumors had started to circulate that we would be leaving soon. Our conversations turned from food to the future. Where would they take us? "Will there be another factory in Germany?" somebody asked. "No!" someone else answered. "It'll be Auschwitz for us. They have enough prisoners in Germany! Their territory's getting smaller, so there are fewer places to work. There's also less food, so the gas chamber is the only place left for us." The majority decision was—no Auschwitz!—even if they did shoot us. Better a bullet than the gas chambers.

And so the days passed. No one did much work. The whole camp was busy unloading the trains laden with sacks of flour arriving from the east.

CHAPTER 26

THE DEATH MARCH

On Friday morning, the nineteenth of January, we were awakened earlier than usual. We were ordered to empty our pillowcases and shown how to turn them into shoulder bags. Each of us received a loaf of bread and a piece of margarine; the red bowl and spoon completed all our possessions. We dressed, got counted and marched from the camp.

It was still dark outside. A light snow was falling, and it was cold. The SS men's wives and children stood shivering in the morning cold. The small four-wheel wagons, loaded to the top with the Germans' possessions, stood in front of the gates: coffers, va-lises, and bedding, just like in 1942, when we were moved into the ghetto. This time, though, it was *die*

Herrenrasse (the "master race"), not the verfluchte Juden.

Despite the fear of what the future held for us, I felt happy. The scene reminded me of the day when all the Jews had been forced to leave their homes and move into the ghetto with only bundles on their backs. I was happy that I was one of the few who were still alive to see the end of Germany. It was a beautiful dream.

A push on my shoulder brought me back to reality. My life was still in the German hands. I was selected to pull one of the wagons. Four of us were hitched to a harness. The women and children sat on top, and we pulled the wagons.

Only a few Germans saw us leave the camp. After we left the city, we headed due west. A feeling of relief came over us. New hope. Maybe we would make it now. This time the SS was running, just like all the other refugees. Auschwitz is east of Gleiwitz.

It started to snow, and it was impossible to walk. The snow started to stick to our wooden shoes, and people started to slip and fall. The soldiers used their whips to help them get up.

Around noon we were permitted to stop and eat our bread. All afternoon we marched, and sometimes we had to run as if the Russians were behind us. Our biggest problem was the snow sticking to our shoes, since we could not stop to knock it off. The

SS men started to get ugly. They shot anyone who slowed down to knock off the snow.

When it got dark, we were brought to an empty camp, and all five hundred of us were pushed into one barn, like sardines in a can. We were made to sit on top of one another's laps, and we could not move all night. People were urinating and defecating wherever they sat. The barracks had no heat, but we were sweating. The door was opened at daybreak, and the cold air enveloped us. We were given hot coffee, then the roll call, and then the second day of the death march started.

It was a clear, cold Saturday morning. The women and children had been taken away during the night. We were made to march without stopping to rest. At noon we passed Neustadt. The sun was shining. We could see Allied prisoners of war clearing bombed-out buildings. Some of the homes were still on fire.

We were all very tired, but the SS pushed us without mercy. Whoever stopped or slowed down was shot and left by the side of the road. Later in the afternoon, we reached the Neisse River. The bridge had been destroyed, and we were trying to get across when a soldier on a motorcycle came racing up the road with orders to turn around. By evening we reached camp Blechhammer, a new name in my collection of camps. Not only was the camp new, but the type of camp was also new to us. All the camps I'd had the displeasure to live in until now had consisted of barracks located in a barbed-wire enclosure. Even Auschwitz had been built that way. But this camp had five-meter-high walls with barbed wire on top and watchtowers with powerful searchlights, just like at Sing-Sing prison. When we walked inside and the gates closed behind us, I had the feeling that we had entered a grave.

When we were brought to the barracks, the people fell into the bunk beds. Despite being without food the whole day, nobody got up when we were told we could get soup. We were supposed to stay in this camp for one day, before our march into Germany. Our legs were as stiff as pieces of wood. During the night, hundreds of prisoners were brought in from other camps.

People started to wake up once it grew light outside. We waited for the usual whistle from the Stubenalteste, but none came. Over the years, we'd been conditioned to wait for an order to leave the barracks, but all was quiet. One of the men sneaked out and came back screaming in Polish, "Neimcy uciekli!" ("The Germans ran away!")

Prisoners started to emerge from the barracks, breaking into the warehouses and looking for food. The SS men, kapos, and the VIPs vanished from the camp without a trace. The gates were locked from the outside.

We were sure this was the end. The camp was waiting for the *Sonderkommandos* (prisoners who were forced to work the death camps) to come and kill us all. Some of the prisoners tried to climb the walls, but to no avail. We walked in circles, with no idea of what to do. Some of us just stood and waited, while others loaded up with items from the stores, grabbing things they knew they would not live long enough to use.

By ten o'clock the gates opened, and a troop of armed SS men walked into the camp. A deadly silence enveloped the thousands of prisoners waiting there. Everybody stood as if frozen in time. We were all waiting to hear the bullets start flying.

I, too, stood there with my eyes closed, imagining the bullets hit my body. The only thoughts passing through my mind were, "Why now?" We had been so close to realizing our dreams. The end was here at last! I suddenly felt somebody pushing me. I opened my eyes and saw the SS men emerging from the storerooms, loaded with food and blankets. They moved toward the gate, hardly paying any attention to us.

Somebody called out, "All the people from Heidelager, step to the gate!" It was Maniek, the foreman at the leather shop at the Heidelager camp, and he recognized an SS officer from there. Maniek made gloves and other leather goods for the SS men's wives, so the two knew each other. After a short conversation, Maniek arranged for the officer to take about two hundred prisoners with him.

People started to run toward the gate, but the SS men counted only two hundred and chased the rest away. Surrounded by the soldiers, we were taken from the camp, and the gates were locked from the outside. My friends Wilek, Lunek, and I made it, as did a few of my other friends.

We were lined up on a side road in rows of four. Surrounded by the soldiers, we awaited the order to march; instead, we heard the sound of a whistle from the main road, and the soldiers started to run. One of the soldiers dropped his backpack and didn't even stop to pick it up.

We stood there, not knowing what to do. Do we march toward the highway, or go back to the camp? Somebody suggested that we march away; another man said, "Maybe the Germans are waiting and will shoot us when we come out."

While we stood in front of the camp debating, a big truck pulled up at the gate. A Polish kapo jumped down and asked us what we were doing outside the camp. After we told him what had happened, he asked if we wanted to go back or walk away. When we saw what they had on the truck, there was no question of what we wanted to do. The bodies of people who had been shot during the death march were stacked there; they'd been brought back to the camp to be burned with the bodies of the other prisoners following the camp's liquidation. We needed no further encouragement and ran in all directions.

Several of us ran across the highway into a wooded area to get our bearings and decide in which direction to go. A Russian woman who was working in the field pointed us toward the east.

We came to a small village but stayed on its perimeter, afraid to be seen by the Germans. They were loading wagons with their possessions. We saw some of our people sneak into a barn, but we decided to stay away.

We went deeper into the woods to find a secluded place to spend the night. A sudden rustling startled us, and we hid in the bushes, thinking the Germans were looking for us. When we saw that they were fellow prisoners, we joined them and, after checking our food supplies, we settled in for the night. Each of us had a loaf of bread and a chunk of frozen margarine. Our assets included a thin prison uniform, a striped coat without a lining, a cap, a pair of shoes with wooden soles, a blanket, a spoon, and a red metal bowl. We talked late into the night about the happenings of the last few days.

I was thinking about my situation. One thing kept reverberating in my mind: "*I am free! I am free!*" So what if the Germans are still around and they're armed. If caught, we would be shot. *But we were free!*

No more barbed wire, barracks, kapos, or SS men. We were now human beings again. We would trade in our numbers for our names again. No more A 17996; it will again be Saul Birnbaum. The dreams of millions who did not make it had come true for me. Here we were, under a moonlit German sky in German woods hiding from the German army— hoping to wake up to a better tomorrow.

CHAPTER 27

IN SEARCH OF THE RED ARMY

The camp was coming to life. People woke up and, after washing themselves in the snow, chewed their frozen bread. Standing in small groups, we asked one another what we should do next. One older man (most of us were young men and boys at the time) got up and called everybody to be quiet. "I was an officer in the Polish army. I don't want to be your leader, but we need one man to give orders. I would like to bring you out of here alive, so listen to me. A lot's happened in the last twenty-four hours. Only yesterday morning, the SS and the kapos were making decisions for us. We are free now, and we have to decide about our future—ourselves. Let's sit down and make some plans."

Another man said, "There is a saying: 'If the mountain won't come to Mohammed, then Mohammed must go to the mountain.' We can't survive here for a week, so we must go and search for the Red Army. Let's line up in rows of four to give the impression that we're prisoners who are being led by the SS guards."

We had started to cross the road when loud voices stopped us in our tracks. We'd just managed to hide in the bushes when a column of German soldiers came into view. It was 1939 and 1941 all over again, only this time, it was the German army instead of the Polish or Russian army, and it felt good to see those "super" soldiers not marching with a song but *schlepping* with their heads down.

They weren't the supermen from 1939. No polished boots and shiny uniforms. They looked as bad as the Polish soldiers had in 1939 and the Russian army in 1941, beaten and demoralized, unshaven, wearing dirty uniforms, some with rags on their feet in place of boots. Seeing them in this condition made our spirits rise. We had actually lived to see the day when the mighty German army would look like that. After they passed, we resumed our march.

German soldiers were setting up anti-aircraft batteries in the fields and paid no attention to us. Our original group of eight decided to separate from the others and start looking for food on our own, because we felt that nobody would be willing to feed fifty people.

We came to a village an hour later, walked into a farmhouse, and asked for some food. They invited us inside and seated us at the table, where we ate the first meal as human beings we'd had in years. They spoke Polish. The house was warm, and we started to talk to our hosts, telling them about all the hard times we'd lived through. The women cried and told us that they did not know anything about concentration camps. It was hard to believe that this could be possible.

This was the first time I'd heard this excuse. Later on, every German I spoke to told me the same story: "Wir hatten Keine Ahnung das Solche Lagern existieren!" ("We had no idea such camps existed!") This was very hard to understand, because there were hundreds of camps all over Germany.

We made ourselves comfortable, freshened up our bread, and sat down to eat. I left the room to go to the outhouse, and while I was sitting there, I saw through the opening in the door the police go inside the house. My heart stopped for a moment, and I sat there perplexed, not knowing what to do. I started to reason with myself, "There's danger in that house—the policeman won't let us leave. He'll probably take us back to Blechhammer. If I run away, how will I be able to stay alive by myself, with no warm clothing or food?"

Resigned to my fate, I walked into the house and heard one of our boys say to the farmer, "Is that what a good Christian is supposed to do? You give us shelter and at the same time you send for a policeman?"

"I didn't send for him," answered the farmer. "He is my brother, and he came to visit me."

Turning to us, the policemen asked, "Which camp did you escape from?"

"We were ordered to go from Blechhammer and report to our old camp in Gleiwitz," one of us answered.

"You probably think I am a *Dummkopf* [simpleton]? They don't let prisoners go free and expect them to return to a camp! You are escapees, and I'll have to take you back to Blechhammer!"

After lengthy pleading with the farmer, we made the policeman agree to take us to Gleiwitz, which was twenty kilometers away. We got dressed and lined up in a double file, with the policeman on a motorcycle behind us. With his rifle at the ready, he told us to march ahead; if we tried anything, he said he would shoot us.

The road led into the woods, and we started to make plans to escape. Speaking quietly, we made a plan to jump him. "He's only one person, and he could shoot one or two of us, but the rest would be saved," we said to one another.

The same idea probably came to him, because he ordered us to stop. He said, "I'm the only policeman in the village, and I can't leave it without protection. You go on to Gleiwitz and report to the police. I'll call them, and if you don't show up there by this evening, they'll search for you." He turned around and drove away.

As soon as he disappeared, we ran into the woods, found a secure place to stay, lay down close to one another, and covered ourselves with our blankets.

That was on Monday evening. We lay quietly and fell asleep. I imagine that's how animals must hibernate. We hardly moved for three days. As if in a daze, I remember getting up once in a while. We had no food or water. Only licking the snow that covered our blankets kept us from dehydration.

We almost gave up and resigned ourselves to die. Some of us even started to recite the prayer for the dying, but on Thursday night, we heard heavy rumbling in the ground and loud explosions in the distance. Our brains, though in a fog from hunger, began to comprehend that liberation was not far away.

On Friday morning we forced ourselves to get up, despite our weakened condition. After a few attempts, we managed to help one another up and, using branches as canes, we walked toward the nearest village. The village wasn't too far away—we could see it beyond the trees—but it took us a long time to get there. Our legs were stiff, and our knees refused to bend. Our wooden shoes kept sliding on the frozen snow, and we kept falling down. It took a lot of willpower to get up again.

The village was almost deserted, although we did see a few old men and women on the road. They directed us to the home of the *Burgermeister* (mayor), which was deserted. The owner had run away, leaving all his possessions behind. Searching for food, we came to the basement. What a sight! We thought we'd died and gone to heaven. Sides of pork, sacks of sugar, barrels of beer, and boxes of *Zwieback* (German cakes) were stacked on shelves. We had started to stuff our mouths with food when a scream jarred us from our feast. A man was yelling at us in Polish to say that the house belonged to the mayor and that he was responsible for it. He told us to leave immediately, but we didn't pay attention to him and kept eating. He left for a while but came back with a German brandishing a gun, and he ordered us to leave.

The commotion brought out other Germans, who offered us food from their homes. We didn't like the idea of being separated and refused to leave the mayor's home. We had a suspicion that they wanted to split us up and then kill us.

The problem was solved when a Russian woman stepped forward and offered to take us all into the farm where she worked. The owner had run away, she said, and the place had enough rooms and food for us all.

When we arrived at the farm, she gave us a hatchet and two plump chickens and told us to chop off their heads and pluck them. In the meantime, she heated pots of water, and we had our first warm bath in years. Soon the heavenly aroma of cooked meat and potatoes filled the house, and we dug into the food with gusto. We finished a couple of loaves of bread, and the pots were soon empty. Our stomachs full and our bodies warm, we went upstairs to sleep but had to get up again very soon. Our intestines had shrunk after being malnourished for such a long time, and the fatty food we'd consumed worked like dynamite. We started a marathon to the outhouse. While one boy was coming up the stairs, another one was running down, with the third one right behind him. The explosions in our stomachs matched the explosions on the horizon. The front was coming near, and we hoped that it would pass us soon.

CHAPTER 28

LIBERATION!

Saturday morning was quiet and sunny. Our hostess asked us to help her clean out the barn. Since the owner had run away, the help had left as well, nobody was left to take care of the cattle.

Into the barn we went. Pitchforks in hand, we started to push the manure into the yard and lay down fresh straw. The work wasn't too pleasant, nor was the smell, but we were grateful to our hostess and felt obligated to her for being so kind to us. While removing the straw, we discovered two Jewish men and a woman hidden underneath. They had been hiding there for a couple of days, they told us, and were very scared and weak. We had to assure them that they were free and that we were awaiting the arrival of the Red Army.

Around ten o'clock, the sun was shining, almost smiling at us as if to say, "Well, children, you made it! After all the hard times, and the camps and ghettos you survived, and soon you'll be free."

It was a quiet morning after a night of heavy fighting all around us. We suddenly heard the clanking of tanks. We ran into the barn and hid under the straw, terror-stricken that the Germans had come back. But soon our fears were assuaged when we heard a *garmoshka* (Russian accordion) in the distance playing a Russian song. We went back to work, impatiently awaiting the arrival of our liberators.

Soon we saw two tanks covered with white sheets, and soldiers in white camouflage clothing stopped near our farm. A woman soldier called me over and asked if we were the owners of the farm. When we explained who we were, she said, "Stop working for Fritz! You are free now!" This was the second time I'd been liberated by the Red Army, and I hoped this time it would be permanent.

Meanwhile, a banquet table was being set up in the house. Vodka, Zwieback, sugar, and other sweets were piled on plates, and everybody was eating and talking at the same time. The noise was earsplitting. The garmoshka played and we sang and danced, unable to believe the nightmare was really over.

In the evening, a Russian major came over to us and started to ask us a lot of questions. After listening to everybody's stories, he advised us to leave as soon as possible. "As you know, the front is not a permanent line," he said. "Sometimes we have to pull back, and I don't think you want to see the Nazis again. You better go to sleep and leave early in the morning. *Rebyata davayte domoy!*" ("Children, go home!")

In the morning we loaded a sled with food. We took a side of salted pork from the mayor's cellar and started out in the opposite direction from where the Russian army was going.

This was Sunday morning, ten days since we'd left Gleiwitz. We were out in the cold again. Sure, we were free, but we weren't safe yet. The road was jammed with Russian tanks, horse-driven wagons, and hundreds of foot soldiers. The whole army was moving west, and we were inching our way east. The soldiers kept asking us, "Skolko kilometrov v Berlin?" ("How many kilometers to Berlin?")

The going was good. The Russians gave us warm army coats and shoes. In a happy mood now, we felt like we were flying, but we soon were brought back down to earth when two German fighter planes started strafing us. Bedlam broke out on the narrow mountain road, with soldiers and horses running in all directions. The screams of wounded horses and humans sounded all around us. The road was strewn with dead bodies. We could see the happy faces of the German pilots every time they came diving down over our heads. A tank was hit by a bomb and burst into flames. We started to run before it exploded.

The man who was pulling our food supplies slipped on the snow and let go of the sled to prevent himself from falling into a ravine. We stood there in horror as we watched our supplies falling down into the abyss. Sorry about our loss but happy to be alive, we ran as far away as possible from that slaughterhouse.

Around noon, we approached two Russian soldiers guarding a grain silo. We asked them for some of the grain. "Who are you?" they asked us.

When we told them that we were Polish, they pointed their guns at us and said, "We're going to shoot you for what you did to our soldiers in 1941. Your people shot at us when we were retreating from the Germans." They started to aim their guns, but then, laughing, they let us go. They still didn't give us any grain, though.

The next time we encountered soldiers, we told them that we were Jewish and got a different reaction. "Hitler killed all the Jews, so if you're still alive, you probably collaborated with the Germans. We'll have to shoot you."

We realized that we were not as safe as we'd thought. From then on, we kept to the side roads and small farms.

One day, we came to an abandoned *Gasthaus* (restaurant). Everything inside was demolished, and the safe had been blown open. Valueless German marks were scattered all over the floor. We used the money to get the stove going so that we could boil some water. Little did we know that only a few months later, after the war ended, it would be legal tender again.

In the evening, we came to a farm and asked for food and a place to sleep. The farmer gave us black coffee and told us that the Russians had taken away all their food.

The family consisted of the farmer and his wife and their two daughters. They were telling us how badly the soldiers had treated them when one of our boys interrupted and said, "What do you have to complain about? You're still alive! Your soldiers not only took our possessions, but they also killed most of our families." That shut them up.

The family gave us a corner in the kitchen to sleep. Happy to be in a warm house, we lay down on the floor. The farmer and his family went into the bedroom and barricaded the door.

After midnight, we heard loud banging on the front door, and a group of Russian soldiers told us to open up. After they searched the house, the soldiers found butter, eggs, *wurst* (salami), and milk and ordered the farmer's wife to fry a few dozen eggs. They asked us who we were and invited us to eat with them.

When the soldiers saw the two young daughters, they made suggestions about taking them to a party. We intervened on their behalf, and the soldiers left without the girls. Before they left, the soldiers told the farmer to treat us well and to thank us for the help. Turning to us, they then said, "You shouldn't sleep on the floor. From now on, you sleep in the bed, and let them sleep on the floor."

We were given the bedroom, and the farmer's family moved into the kitchen. But the bed was too soft and the covers too warm for us, so we spent the night sleeping on the floor.

In the morning, after a good breakfast—now the family had found a lot of food for us—the farmer offered us a deal. If we stayed and worked for a few weeks on the farm, he would feed us and pay us a good salary. He really wanted us for security, because he expected us to keep his family safe from the Russians. We declined his offer, though, since we were in too much of a hurry to get home.

CHAPTER 29

GOING HOME

U sing all kinds of locomotion, we inched our way east. We used army trucks and empty ammunition and coal trains, or we just marched. We slept in apartments vacated by fleeing Germans.

The first Polish town we came to was Czestochowa. A lot of the Jews in the town had been saved in the nick of time by the Russians. The SS men were loading the Jews into cattle cars for transport to Germany when the Red Army slipped quietly into town and, after a fierce street fight, took the town and freed all the prisoners. The Germans managed to send two trainloads away before the Russians arrived. The poor souls were so close to being liberated. I spoke to a few people who'd survived the transports, and they told me of the terrible things that had happened to them before their liberation by the Allies. The Jewish Committee gave us some money and told us that we'd better go home. We didn't need any encouragement, so we caught an ammunition train and left town.

In the small town of Staszow, we found out for the first time after our liberation that the old Polish hatred of the Jews had not diminished with the end of Nazism. We went to the police station and asked for a place to sleep. The room was filled with liberated prisoners from all the nations of Europe. The policemen were very helpful to them. When they found out that we were Jews, they handed us over to a policeman, who escorted us to an abandoned camp far from town. We refused to stay there and were ready to attack the policeman. Only then did he agree to take us back to the police station. When we told them that we would complain to the Russian authorities, they relented and took us to an apartment in the city.

The apartment was occupied by a woman and her two daughters. The policeman ordered them to give us some food and a place to sleep. Crying, the woman told us that her family had been persecuted by the police because her husband was a *Volksdeutcher* (of German ancestry).

We left in the morning for the railroad station. When we told the people where we'd spent the night, they burst out in laughter. The funny part of the story was that the poor, persecuted family had actually been the wife and daughters of a high-ranking Gestapo officer. He'd escaped, leaving the family behind.

A coal train took us some distance, and we had to get off at a small railroad station. We spent three days there among hundreds of people waiting for a train. Until this time, we'd been lucky to avoid being infested with lice. Here, however, sleeping on the floor without washing facilities, we weren't so lucky and would not be able to rid ourselves of the pests until we got home.

An overloaded train eventually arrived, and we found a spot on the roof. The train stopped after a short ride, and the passengers were told to get off and cut down trees and wooden fences; otherwise, we would not be able to continue. The locomotive had run out of firewood. After we collected enough wood, the train moved again. It took four weeks of getting on and off trains before we finally approached our town. By that time, only three of the original eight of us were left. The others had departed along the way.

With great excitement, we boarded the final train that would take us to our hometown, Przemysl. I recognized a costumer from our grocery business before the war and asked him about the town. To my question "How many Jews are left?" he answered,

"There are plenty of Jews! Hitler didn't kill them all." That was a hell of a welcome. I'd expected a warm embrace after all the terrible things that had happened to us. I still had hopes that the others would behave differently.

The long-awaited moment finally arrived. I was home. The gates of the railroad station opened, and we walked into the familiar streets we hadn't seen since 1942, when the ghetto was first established.

The first stop was the Jewish Committee, where we received the bad news. Only two hundred Jews were left of the seventeen thousand who had lived in the town before the war. There were others, but they had come from other towns.

I leafed through the registration books but could not find any of the names I was looking for. I knew that my mother and sister had been taken away during the first Umsiedlung in 1942 and had been sent to the Belzec liquidation camp. My father had been shot by the Gestapo and buried in a mass grave in 1943. I still had hope that my younger brother had somehow survived in one of the camps.

The Jewish Committee gave us a little money and a temporary apartment. Wilek, Lunek, and I, in very low spirits after all our fantasies about our homecoming, started to look for jobs, but there were none. We tried our luck at peddling. We walked all day from house to house, selling shoelaces, toothpaste, and other small items, but we could not make a living. We were warned not to step outside of town, because they were still killing Jews. Lunek couldn't even go to see a farmer to reclaim a dining-room set his family had left for safekeeping.

The Polish underground army (armia Krajowa, or AK) and the Ukrainian Banderowcy—followers of General Bandera, who collaborated with the Nazis—were fighting each other, but they seemed to agree on one thing, which was killing Jews in order to take their money. The Russians were grabbing people in the streets and sending them to the front line to fight, without any training.

In order to avoid being caught, we registered with the Polish army and received a month's rest before reporting for duty.

There was no place for a Jew in Poland in the year 1945. Everywhere we looked, we were reminded of the terrible happenings that were still going on. Every foot of ground was soaked with Jewish blood. Most of our homes had been destroyed or taken over by the Poles, and all our families and friends were gone. All the evidence of hundreds of years of Jewish history had been burned out. The populace hated us because we had survived and they would now have to give us back our stolen property.

Lunek and I decided to leave Poland. Wilek fell in love and was ready to settle down, so he stayed. We'd heard rumors about a secret organization called the Brichah ("escape" or "flight") that was smuggling Jews to Palestine, so we set out to find them.

By the end of March, we were ready to leave the town we had dreamed about during all those long nights in the concentration camps. The town of the happy days of our youth. It was now the town of bad memories, of the ghetto, the Gestapo, the SS, and the Sonderkommandos whose purpose it was to kill Jews.

EPILOGUE

The group of forty-two people we'd separated from on the morning after our escape returned to our old camp in Gleiwitz without any incident and were liberated by the Russians. The ten people who hid in the German village were discovered in the barn and killed. Only one survived by hiding under a pile of hay.

The Germans returned on Monday to camp Blechhammer and took all the prisoners to Germany. The majority died during the march or were killed in the camps. Some survived and were liberated by the British and Americans.

Wilek and Lunek settled in Israel, and I settled in Brooklyn, New York. I eventually moved to Boca Raton, Florida, where I wrote this book.

END OF BOOK ONE

PART TWO

The Brichahnik

CHAPTER 1

THE FLIGHT FROM POLAND

Barely two months after our return from the concentration camp, we were getting ready to leave Poland. We'd heard rumors that the Brichah was smuggling Jews out of Poland. Our job was to find the organization. Somehow, we failed to get in touch with anybody who could give us any information about how to locate the group.

Lunek and I decided to go out and find them on our own. The biggest problem was our lack of money. One of my father's friends, Mr. Penner, gave me two thousand zlotys, and I sold a fur coat my mother had left with a Christian neighbor. With the help of a friend who was in the militia, Lunek was able to get back the dining-room set his family had left with a farmer. We were able to buy two ID cards with the money. Lunek became a Greek Jew, and I a Romanian Jew by the name of Abraham Forkas.

For a bottle of vodka, we were able to get a ride on a Russian army truck to Rzeszow. After a two-day search, we came up with nothing. Nobody knew anything about that elusive organization. A man at the Jewish Committee told us to go to the railroad station and look for groups of young people, and we would probably find what we were looking for.

We took his advice and, after boarding a train, we found what we thought was our connection. In one of the compartments we saw a group of boys and girls. We tried to engage them in conversation, but they refused to talk to us. We left the compartment but decided to stay close to them, no matter where they went.

When we saw that the group was ready to leave the train, we kept close to them. They left the train at the station in Jaslo, and we followed right behind them.

Jaslo! What terrible memories. That had been my first station on the way to hell in 1943. From this station, we were chased to camp Szebnie. This time, Lunek and I took a horse and wagon, and we traveled in the opposite direction, to the city of Jaslo.

It was a five-kilometer ride into town. We stayed on their tail and followed them block after block, afraid to lose them. We knew that they were our only link to that elusive organization. They eventually arrived at their destination. They stopped in front of a two-story building, and one of them went inside. He returned after a while with another man. The man came over to us and in a tough voice said, "You guys better leave before we break your bones." After this warning, he and the group walked away, leaving us standing in the middle of the street.

We didn't have the slightest idea what to do next. What could we do in a strange town? Where could we go? Finally we decided that I would stay and watch the building, while Lunek would go to get help from the Jewish Committee.

It was getting chilly, so I walked inside the building and sat down on the stairs. I must have dozed off after a while. I don't know how long I slept, but I was awakened by a loud noise as if the building were collapsing on top of me. I jumped up and saw a giant running down the stairs. He was well over six feet tall and probably weighed 250 pounds. When he stood in front of me, I had to look up to see his face.

We stood there looking at each other, and we screamed at the same time. He yelled, "Siolek!" and I yelled "Metz!" Then we stood staring unbelievingly at the other. Yes, this had been my best friend in the ghetto. We used to go out together with our girlfriends, only to be separated in camp Szebnie in November 1943.

He took me up to the place he shared with his aunt, and when I told him my dilemma, he assured me not to worry, because the whole leadership of the Brichah was eating at his aunt's house.

I went down, and when Lunek returned empty-handed, I told him the good news. He would not believe it and said that I had lost my marbles. I myself could hardly believe our good fortune. Things like that usually happened only in the movies. One minute we had no hope; the next, the future looked bright and rosy.

First we ate. And how we ate. Our last meal had been an early breakfast, in Rzeszow. We talked late into the night, reliving the nightmare, and then we went to sleep with a promise that in the morning, Metz would fix everything.

Over breakfast, he introduced us to the leadership of the Brichah, and they told us to leave immediately for the railroad station, where a group was getting ready to leave for the Czech border. We wouldn't be able to join the group until we crossed the Polish border, but they gave us a letter for the transport leader that explained the situation.

We put on our camp uniforms and took off for the railroad station. Out of breath, we ran into the station, but we were too late. When I asked the two militiamen in German if they'd seen "Meine Kameraden," (My friends) one of them pointed to the tracks and said, "Cameraden poof poof, weg." Turning to the other policeman, he said in Polish, "Poor guy. His friends left without him, and he doesn't speak Polish." Back at the apartment, we were told not to worry. We would have to try again the following morning.

We woke up very early and arrived at the railroad station before the others. The transport leader had been informed about us, and he told us to stay with them.

As our luck would have it, no train was in sight; to our inquiries, we received the standard answer: "Who knows? We'll know when the train arrives." So we waited and waited, until in the late afternoon, a long transport train stopped at the station. The train, surrounded by Russian soldiers, consisted of ten passenger cars and a large number of cattle cars, flatcars, and boxcars. It was a resettlement train on its way to Siberia. The Russians were resettling a whole Ukrainian village because they'd collaborated with the Germans: men, women, and children; farm animals and machinery; furniture, straw, and hay.

When we found out that the train was going to Sanok, which was close to the Czech border, we climbed on top of a car loaded with hay and settled in for the ride. The Ukrainians tried to chase us off, but we would not budge. They called the guards and told them that we were Germans. The only language we were told to use was Hebrew, but many of our people spoke Yiddish, which sounds a lot like German.

It was dark by the time the Russians came over to us, demanding our papers. We pretended that we didn't understand Russian and that we didn't know what they wanted from us.

Now please picture a scene like this. It was dark, and we were sitting on top of the hay wagon. The soldiers had encircled the car we were on. One of the soldiers climbed up, and we had a conversation. "Give me your papers!"

One of us answered in Hebrew, "Anee lo mayveen." ("I don't understand.")

"Your documents, please! Who are you? Polish? Jewish?"

"Anee Yehudee" ("I am Jehudee") was the answer.

"There is no such nation," the soldier said.

We saw that the soldier was getting impatient, so the transport leader took out our permits and gave them to the Russian. It was too dark to read, so he asked, "Who has a match?" Nobody answered. The soldier tried to make us understand in sign language. He mimed putting a cigarette into his mouth and lighting it. One of our boys gave him a cigarette, lit it for him, and put the matches back into his own pocket. The soldier grabbed the matches, lit one, and started to read the papers. They were in Russian and were all in order, with lots of red stamps. They stated "These former concentration camp prisoners are permitted to return to their homelands, and we order all military personnel to give them all possible help to assure them a safe return home." They were signed by army headquarters, with two round and one triangular stamp. The more stamps on a Russian document, the more impressive and convincing it is. It was the best. It was the best the Brichah could make.

After all the commotion, the soldiers told the Ukrainians to let us stay on the train until we reached the border. At a station near the border, we left the train and took one that was headed toward the Czechoslovakian border.

By the morning, the train was chugging up and down the Carpathian Mountains, through the Dukla Pass. What a magnificent view! As far as the eye could see were high peaks covered with snow, some of them hiding in the clouds. The sun made the snow sparkle as if the mountains were covered with diamonds. After we crossed the border, we ripped up our Polish IDs and threw them into the wind, to be blown all over the mountains.

CHAPTER 2

ON THE WAY TO PALESTINE

Our first town across the border was Humana. We stayed in the Red Cross shelter there for two days until new papers were produced for us, at which point we became members of the group. We were split into two groups: Greeks and Yugoslavs. This was a precaution. In case real Greeks came looking for their compatriots, we would all become Yugoslavs. The same would happen if Yugoslavs came: we would all become Greeks.

One day an older Jewish man came to us and asked, "Where are you from, children?"

We answered, "From Salonika."

"Salonika? Is that near Lemberg?" he said, referring to Lviv, Poland. We could not fool him.

Our complete Greek lexicon consisted of *ka-limera*, *kalisfera*, and *kalinichta* (good morning, good afternoon, and good night). The only ones among us who were permitted to speak were those who knew Hebrew. We had the honor of seeing Edvard Beneš, the president of Czechoslovakia, and then we had to leave. Our next stop was Budapest, Hungary.

We spent a few days in a school and wandered around the two river cities of Buda and Pest, joined by bridges across the Danube. Many beautiful buildings were still smoldering, and the streets were littered with debris from bombed-out buildings. The metro was still operating and a few stores were open, but most of them had been burned out, or their doors splintered and their merchandise looted.

Every day at noon we were taken to a restaurant, where we were introduced to paprika. Everything was drowned in paprika. Chicken soup is supposed to be golden, correct? In Budapest it was red, as was the meat. The food was so spicy that we drank gallons of water or beer during and after every meal.

As nice as it was there, the time eventually came for us to leave. Our next stop was Tokay, famous for its wine. We had a doctor in our group, who prescribed that we drink as much of the wine as possible. "Every glass of this wine will add a year to your life," he said. So we kept drinking; if he was right, we expected to be healthy for many years.

It was the first night of Passover, and we spent the first Seder with a Jewish family. We retold the story of our liberation from the camps amid many tears. They told us how the town had been taken by the Russians, many of whom had drowned in the gigantic wine barrels set up in the caves to age the wine. The soldiers had climbed over the top and had fallen in. What a way to die!

In the morning, the bakery gave each of us a loaf of bread. The bread was white, round, and large—as large as a car wheel. We had to wrap the loaves in blankets and carry them over our shoulders.

At the edge of town, we met the first Romanian soldiers we'd seen, manning a military checkpoint. This was the only place to acquire transportation to the nearest railroad station. While we were waiting, we saw a group of people coming toward us, and we were sure they were genuine Greeks. We got ready to leave before they approached us, because we'd told the soldiers we were Greeks; if they talked to us, we'd be in trouble.

They, too, stopped when they saw us, until somebody said *amchu*—Hebrew for "our nation"—and they answered *amchu*, and then we knew they were the same Greeks we were. Just another Brichah unit looking for transportation.

We left together when a military transport came by. They dropped us off at the rail station in Ny-iregyhaza. After waiting a few hours with no sign of a train, we sent two boys into town to find other Jews. A little while later, two local boys came over and asked for the Greeks. As usual, we said that we were Yugoslavs. They left, only to return later to tell us that our friends were waiting at the synagogue. We picked up our belongings and went with them. Because it was the second night of Passover, all the Jews were in the synagogue, and since many of them had just returned to their homes from the Budapest ghetto, they held a communal Seder.

The transport leaders told us not to speak to the local people, for fear of being discovered. Only a few of our group (those who were fluent in Hebrew) were permitted to speak, and it was very hard to converse with the local Jews. Our people spoke modern (Sephardi) Hebrew, but our companions spoke biblical Hebrew (Ashkenazi). After the meal, the local Hebrew teacher got up and spoke. "Look at those young people. It is a pleasure to hear them speak the language of our forefathers. For you, it is a holy language, to be used only for prayer. For you, it is a dead language, but they make it come to life."

We were invited to spend the night in their homes, but we decided to stay together, so we spent the night in the synagogue. In the morning, after breakfast, we left for the railroad and made it to Debrecen.

At that time, people traveled mostly in boxcars. Sometimes we had to travel on the roofs of the cars. We did that very often when we had no money to buy railroad tickets. Outside the station, the peddlers were selling yellow cakes. Being hungry, we bought some, but we threw them away as soon as we tasted them. They were just corn cakes, with no taste at all. That was my introduction to *mamaliga*.

As had happened many times before, no trains were leaving the station. The American Joint Distribution Committee (AJDC, or simply "Joint") had given each of us some money, but they could not provide transportation across the border. One of our companions, a very tall man named Chanina (whom I will talk about later), made a deal with the station-master. For a certain amount of money, he would rent us a locomotive with a crew to get us close to the Romanian border. As soon as it got dark, we climbed all over the locomotive, standing on any foothold we could find, and away we went. It was a wild ride. The crew wanted to make the trip as quickly as possible and didn't care how many passengers they lost along the way. We in turn held on to anything we could grab. The locomotive ran without lights and at high speed. The wind hit our faces and whistled past our ears. Somewhere along the road, we hit an obstacle of some kind. We could feel the impact, but the engineer did not stop to look.

Something soft flew against us, and since we were in Transylvania now, we were sure that they were bats. Later we discovered later that they were bundles of tobacco leaves that somebody had tried to smuggle across the border and had flown loose. The cigarettes we made from those leaves lasted us a long time.

We got off in the small village of Pispeklodany, not far from the Romanian border. We couldn't believe that we'd all survived that hellish ride. Tired and scared, with our faces burning from the wind, we climbed down from the locomotive. Our appearance would be hard to imagine today. We were all covered with soot and grease, and it took a long time for us to get cleaned up. After we had something to eat, we went to sleep, but we had to get up before sunup. A border guide took us across the Romanian border. The crossing was easy, and at daybreak we found ourselves on a train headed to Oradea. A day's rest, and we were on our way to Cluj. This was the city from which our people had taken the express train to Bucharest. From there, the route led to the Black Sea, and then by boat to Turkey and Palestine.

CHAPTER 3

THE MYSTERY OF THE MISSING CHANINA

A funny incident comes to mind about the man Chanina I mentioned earlier. On our way from Oradea to Cluj, we took a transport train loaded with empty ammunition boxes. We all found places to sit down among the boxes. When night came, some of the people climbed into the boxes and went to sleep. About midnight, we heard a scream from Chanina's wife: "Chanina is missing!"

So were the boxes where he'd been sleeping. We had no way to stop the train. It was not a passenger train, and there were no emergency cords to pull, so we couldn't do anything but wait for the next stop.

We were sure he was dead, likely crushed beneath the wheels of the train. Imagine our surprise when we pulled into the station at Cluj, and there he was, all seven feet of him, alive and well. When the excitement was over, he told us a funny and unbelievable story.

"I went to sleep in a box and didn't see how close I was to the edge. I woke up feeling cold and wet, lying on the grass. I was momentarily too stunned to realize what had happened, but after a while, I understood that I'd fallen off the train, and the empty boxes had saved my life. I'd rolled down the embankment, and the rain woke me up.

"I started to walk along the track, hoping to come to a station, but after a few hundred yards, the rails divided. I stood there for a while, not knowing which direction to take.

"Looking around me, I saw a blinking light in the distance, so I started to walk toward it. The light was coming from a farmhouse. The door was locked, so I had to climb in through an open window. The farmer's family awakened from sleep and mistook me for a Russian.

"The woman fell to her knees, begging me in her language, while the man tried to slip away, but I grabbed him and started to drag him toward the barn. Pointing to the horse and wagon, I tried to tell him in a mixture of Polish, Russian, and German that he should take me to Bucharest, but he didn't understand. I hitched the horse to the wagon and, using sign language and something that sounded like *mregee Bucharesti*, made the farmer get his coat, and we were ready to start out.

"Before we started out, the woman handed something to her husband. Suspecting a gun, I snatched it away from him, only to find a bottle of vodka. After having a good swallow from the bottle, I ordered him to go.

"We traveled for almost an hour—he slowed down every once in a while, and I made him go faster—until at last we came to a highway. He stopped the wagon and started to tell me something that I didn't understand. The only words I could hear were *soldati* and *Bucharesti*. After waiting for a while, a transport of soldiers came by. We stopped them, and I started to speak in German, hoping that somebody would understand me. One of the officers did understand what I'd said, and I told him my story, imploring him to get in touch with the railroad stations along the way.

"We drove to a nearby station and found out that a transport train was on its way to Cluj. The officer took pity on me and drove me in his car to the railroad station in Cluj before the train came in. And that's where I was when you came looking for me."

CHAPTER 4

STUCK IN ROMANIA

The Brichah gave us tickets for the express train, and we waited for the next train. Ten people were leaving Cluj at a time, but by the time my leave had come, trouble had developed. The Russians had closed all the Black Sea ports, and the whole movement of our transports throughout Romania stalled. We returned our tickets, were put up in a hotel, and waited for future developments.

While we waited in the hotel, we had a very bad experience that brought back memories of the Nazi period. We were careful not to speak Yiddish or Polish in public, but in the privacy of our hotel room, we spoke Yiddish. Someone among the hotel workers overheard us, and thinking we were speaking German, called the NKVD. The secret police came into our room, accused us of being Nazis, and told us that we were under arrest. When we told them that we were Jewish, they demanded that we show them if we were circumcised. Because our group included a few girls, all the boys had to go with the Russians to the next room and drop their pants. The Germans used the same method of identification as proof of someone being Jewish. Only Jews were circumcised in Europe at that time. After the Russians were convinced that we were indeed Jewish, they went away and left us alone.

Bucharest was overcrowded, so the Brichah began to open *kibbutzim* (a communal farm) all over Romania. Our group was sent to the small town of Ocna Mures, in the vicinity of the larger city of Alba Iulia.

We again changed our nationalities. "From now on," we were told, "you are Polish Jews, liberated from concentration camps in Hungary and staying here until you recuperate." We were also told that the Jews in Mures were very religious and that we would have to behave accordingly.

The first problem we encountered was hats and skullcaps. Orthodox Jews keep their heads covered at all times, especially when they eat or enter a synagogue, and the majority of us did not have either. We used the excuse that we had been riding on the roofs of trains, and the wind had blown them off.

It was the last day of Passover, and here, too, the Jews ate their meals in the synagogue. We had to wait outside until the local kids could bring us hats from their homes. Only in the United States does every temple provide skullcaps for the congregation. It was not done that way in the old country, because everybody wore a hat. We were seated at a long table, and we ate together with the townspeople. After we were finished, we had to answer many questions. The rabbi listened to our stories and promised to give us all the help he could.

We spent that night in the homes of various townspeople, and on the following day, a large house on the outskirts of town was rented to us, and we moved in. In the beginning, they cooked all our meals in town and brought it back by horse and wagon. After a while, though, they built a big stove in the basement, and a local woman watched to make sure that our girls adhered to the kosher dietary laws. A *mashgiach* (one who oversees the kosher status of food) supplied our food, which he bought at the marketplace. All this was paid for by the Joint.

Every morning, the men and boys went to synagogue to pray. Every Friday evening and Saturday after the prayers, we were invited to the homes of the local Jews for meals. Saturday afternoons were visiting times in our kibbutz. All the men, women, and children, along with their maids, came to us, and we had to entertain them. We did not mind singing Hebrew songs or dancing, but we could not accept the constant surveillance by the little ones, whom their parents had put up to watch us to make sure that our boys didn't walk away with the local girls.

Not all our people were religious, and they had to hide if they wanted to smoke a cigarette, which is forbidden on Saturdays.

Life in the kibbutz started to settle into a routine: Hebrew lessons for beginners, advanced courses for those who knew some of the language. The Brichah kept sending more people, because the transports kept coming from Poland and there was no place else to go. World War II was still on. Germany was almost finished, but it was still fighting. On the thirteenth of April, the Russians took Vienna. On the twenty-fifth of the same month, US and Russian troops met at Torgau, Germany. Still, the Germans fought on harder than before, but their strongholds fell one by one until finally there was only Berlin.

We had to look for a larger place, so we rented a damaged building and made a deal with the owner. In exchange for repairing the building, we would have the right to use it as long as we needed it without paying rent. We had nothing to do, so both sides were happy with the deal.

Life in our kibbutz changed with the influx of new people. After spending long years in concentration camps, the young people now refused to have anything to do with religion. One by one, they stopped attending the morning prayers; after a while, only the older people went to synagogue.

The new management found out that they could buy produce directly from the farmers for much less. They made a deal directly with the butcher to bring us the hind parts of the lambs at night, which had more meat than the forepart. Up until now, the mashgiach had been delivering the front part of the lambs, which was kosher. The hind part has an artery that has to be removed in order to make it kosher. This procedure has to be done by a specialist, and very few small towns could afford one in the old country.

When the rabbi found out about all the sins we were committing—including smoking cigarettes on the Sabbath—he declared our place to be off limits to the Jewish community. He called in our leadership and admonished them for breaking the Jewish laws and for being a bad influence on the young people of the town. Angry words were exchanged, and our friendly relations with the Jews of the village came to an end.

Some of us got jobs loading salt. The town had a few salt mines, where we sometimes worked up above if they had extra work to be done. I became very friendly with a man named Yojnale, and we got a job as night watchmen, making a few extra leus, the Romanian currency. Lunek got a job in the kibbutz management and became a big shot, but two girls from Przemysl named Sara and Tusia were still with us, so I was not alone.

The girls also helped me a lot when I became very sick one time. It was a baffling malady, and our doctor couldn't diagnose the disease. Each Wednesday, my temperature shot up to 42 degrees Celsius (107 degrees Fahrenheit); it stayed that way for twenty-four hours, and then it suddenly disappeared without a trace, and I would be back to normal until the following Wednesday. This went on for a couple of weeks, so the doctor made an appointment in my name at a hospital in Alba Iulia.

Before I went in to my appointment, though, something very important happened. Something we had all hoped for, but very few had lived to see. On May first, the suicide of Hitler was announced, and on the second day of May, Berlin fell to the Russians. The newspaper headline read on the seventh of May, V-E Day! Germany Surrenders at Reims, France.

The bells tolled and the sirens wailed, announcing peace to all the people.

CHAPTER 5

THE WAR ENDS—WE'RE ON THE MOVE AGAIN

Peace came at last. There were parades and dancing in the streets. We marched and sang all the Russian songs we knew. The mayor of the city put us in the front lines of the parade. There were parties all over town, and we were the main attraction.

One day finally, the party was over, and we returned to our daily routine. Our overexposure at the victory parades had not done us any good. The NKVD became interested in us, so we received a few visits in which they inquired about our plans for the future. We really had to make a fast decision. The same thing was happening all over Romania, so the Brichah decided to move us out. We were on the move again.

My temperature was still rising every Wednesday, so the doctor told me to go to the hospital for tests before we left. "Who knows where your next chance to go to a hospital will be," he told me. So one morning in June, I got up and walked to the crossroads, where a farmer took me with his horse and wagon to Alba Iulia.

It was a small hospital, and I spent one week there, going through all kinds of tests. The food was excellent. Every day for breakfast, lunch, and dinner, mamaliga. After the third day, I was sick and tired of mamaliga. When my friend Yojnale came to visit me, I begged him to buy me some bread and butter, but the store owner would not sell anything to a "piskosz lengel zsido" ("dirty Polish Jew"). This was the first time I'd heard this expression, but it would not be the last. Someone later explained this hatred to me. It was their memories from the camps.

By the time the Hungarian Jews arrived in Auschwitz in June 1944, the polish Jews were already old hands at the camp game. They were the kapos, foremen, and Stubenaltestes, and some of them gave the newcomers a hard time. They did that to everybody. I remembered that when we arrived there, we'd received the same treatment from our compatriots. That was the name of the game there. The one who was holding the stick was breaking the heads of those who didn't have sticks. So it was the "piskosz langel zsido" who gave them a hard time.

After one week's stay in the hospital and passing through a whole battery of tests, I knew as much about my ailment as I'd known when I'd gone in. I never did find out what had been wrong with me, or why my temperature spiked on Wednesdays.

CHAPTER 6

TWO JEWS, THREE PARTIES

When I got back to the kibbutz, the atmosphere was very tense. Many people had left and were on their way to Austria. People were leaving according to the groups they belonged to. We were no longer Jews; now we were Hashomer, Hanoar, Gordonia, and many other parties.

First there was the Yichida, or United, which was organized by those who'd come from the concentration camps, the woods, and from various hiding places. They said, "We are all Jews, and we all want to go to Israel, so let's forget all the petty fights and all the different parties. Let's unite, because in unity there is strength."

The Jews were members of many different parties before the war. A common saying at the time was "Two Jews, three parties." Among others, there were the Hashomer on the left, and the Hanoar on the right. There were the Agudah (Hasidic), the Mizrachi (religious), the Gordonia (socialist), and we can't forget the Bethar (revisionists) with their brown uniforms. There were splinter groups of big parties and splinter groups of the splinter groups. With the coming of Hitler, however, all party affiliations ceased to exist. For Hitler and his henchmen, a Jew was a Jew, no matter which party he belonged to. Jewish communists went to the gas chambers with Jewish fascists. So those of us who came back from the camps—the Sherah Ha'pleyta, the survivors of the Holocaust—decided to forget all party ideologies and become one. We were all just Jews.

In May 1945, as soon as the war ended, the old party game started again. The *shlichim* (messengers) from Israel came to us with greetings from the old parties. The party system had continued unabated there, and they came to look for their leftover members.

I'd been in this kibbutz for three months, and we'd never asked anyone which party they belonged to. I found out that seven others were also from Gordonia, my old organization. We started to leave in groups, and finally, my time to leave arrived. I'd become separated from Lunek. He was part of the Hanoar party, and I was Gordonia. And so, after all we'd gone through together in the camps and during our escape from camp and from Poland, we were forced to go our separate ways. I lost all trace of him after this.

Our group had arrived here as Polish Jews, but when we left, we took Austrian identities. We'd stayed long enough to learn the history of the Austrian Jews. We'd need to know the names of our designated hometowns, when we'd left for the camps, the streets where we'd lived, and anything else we needed to know about Austria. The Brichah workers tested us again and again until we knew the history of the Jews in Austria. Anyone who did not memorize his history lesson was left behind until he learned.

When I knew all about Salzburg, the town the new me had come from, I was shipped out with a group that was leaving for Austria. We crossed the border into Hungary and traveled north by our regular means of transportation: cattle cars or flatcars, and sometimes on the roofs of passenger trains, depending on the weather.

The trip was slow and the weather mostly good, so we took our time getting to Budapest. The towns along the way were very picturesque, with homes covered with clinging vines. Looking out from the open doors of the trains, we could see for miles and miles the flat grasslands of the Hungary. The water at every stop tasted differently. One town where we stopped had carbonated water coming from the pumps, and we were told that it was very healthy. People used to come from all over the world to drink it. When we stopped at another station for a short while, a group of kids sold us bottles of water, and when we tried to drink some, we had to spit it out. It tasted of rotten eggs—good for mineral baths, but not for drinking. The smell stayed with us for a long time. We spent two days in Budapest and were sent with a larger group to Sopron, Hungary. In Sopron, the group was split up and sent in two directions. One would travel to Vienna, and the other to Graz. Vienna was my destination, a flatcar my transportation. Our first stop in Austria was Wiener Neustadt, where we had our first encounter with Germans since our escape from camp Blechhammer.

"Kommen Sie herunter, schnell!" That was the shout I had not expected to hear ever again. It opened old wounds, and bad memories. I would never have dreamed seven months before, when I'd escaped from the camps, that I would ever again step on the forsaken soil of Germany—and of my own free will, no less. But here I was, listening to a German screaming at me once again.

The conductor asked for tickets, which we didn't have. He spoke German, and we answered in Yiddish. He asked for papers, and when he saw that we were Austrians, he asked us why we didn't speak German, to which we answered, "No more German for us. That is the language of the killers of our dear ones, and we've made a promise never to speak it again." He turned around and walked away.

We arrived in Vienna and were taken to a school on Schlaghoff Strasse. This was a transit camp of the Brichah. Only half the building was occupied by our people; the other half was occupied by the wives and children of SS men who'd been sent to Siberia.

Vienna was under Russian occupation in July 1945, and it was very difficult to get out larger transports into the American occupation zone. To reach the Americans, the transport had to travel through a hundred kilometers of Russian-occupied territory under constant danger of being discovered. As a result, small groups of only ten people each were able to leave for the border.

While waiting for an order to leave, we spent time visiting the neighborhood. To be in Vienna and not be able to see the famed city was a real disappointment, but we were forbidden to wander too far from our camp. We had to walk to a nearby restaurant to get our meals, while the local population stood outside, waiting for our leftovers.

CHAPTER 7

A JOURNEY TO THE AMERICAN ZONE

Our train left the Vienna Westbahnhof at midnight. We had tickets and were riding inside like normal people. Hundreds of refugees from all the nations of Europe were on the train, which was moving very slowly. We had to stop very often and move to sidings, because there was only one rail. Most of the rails had been destroyed by Allied bombers. Klein Pöchlarn was the last station on this line; anything past that town was in shambles.

We left the train and took a ferry across the Danube to Gross Pöchlarn, where we had to take a train to Mauthausen. When we got off the ferry, we walked into a sea of people. The station and the surrounding fields were covered with people, all waiting for a train that never came.

We looked for our people, and when we shout-ed the word "amchu," about forty people answered our call. These were our people from four previous transports; the four groups of ten people plus our group made it fifty. Not far from the station was a small mountain where grapes were grown, but we saw bunches of people instead of grapes. The terrac-es in which rows of grapevines had once grown were now covered with a mass of humanity—if you could call it humanity. Most of them looked like zombies, walking around with glassy eyes as they looked for a bit of food. But there was none. No train came by on this side for a week, but people kept coming to Klein Pöchlarn, and the ferry kept bringing them across the river.

We ate our food supplies at first, but later we start-ed to strip the nearby fields of all the crops, since we were afraid to wander too far and thus miss the train. But hunger made us walk farther and farther, eating everything in sight. Like a plague of locusts, we cleaned up the surrounding fields. The farmers came after us with sticks and pitchforks but were un-able to accomplish anything. There were hundreds of us, and we were desperate.

And then one morning, the train came. It was already filled with people. We ran down the moun-tain like an avalanche. Instead of snow, though, it was a black mass of humanity now moving toward the train, and in no time it was impossible to see the train. All anybody could see was people hanging on to anything they could grab. From the mountainside it looked like a column of ants. The train crew tried to chase us away, but we kept coming back. After a while they gave up.

The train started to chug along very slowly, which was lucky for some of the people who were losing their grip and starting to fall. The train stopped in a field late in the afternoon, and we were told to get off. This was the border.

Hundreds of people left the train and started to run up a hill. We collected our people and waited for someone named Robert, our man in Mauthausen. The group leaders waved blue handkerchiefs as a signal for Robert, but nobody came.

We had no time to lose. The others were almost on top of the hill, and we had to decide what to do. Do we go ahead or turn back and wait for Robert? One of our boys said, "I'll take you! I've been on the other side a few times. Let's go! We just have to walk over that hill, and on the other side are the Amis" (the Americans).

We'd made it to the bottom of the hill but were still in a field of high wheat when a volley of machine-gun fire passed over our heads. The others ran back. We dropped to the ground and just lay there. It was the Russian border patrol. They had to be stupid or blind not to have seen such a mob trying to get through. Nobody was shot. They were not trying to kill anybody.

Before it got dark, they rounded everyone up. We were surrounded by Russian soldiers, who told us to lie down in the wheat field and warned us not to run, because they would shoot to kill. We spent the night in that field.

The guards woke us up at daybreak and started us on a march, away from the border. It reminded me of January 1945, the only difference being that this was Ruskies instead of SS men. They were taking us to a camp of some kind, and we were afraid we would wind up in Siberia.

After a two-hour march, we stopped for a rest on the highway, near a farm. As I was sitting there, I saw a couple of Germans among us walk over to a guard and talk to him, pointing toward a barn. The guard shook his head yes, and the two Germans walked to the barn, let down their pants, and squatted, inching their way behind the barn. Once they were out of sight of the soldier, they pulled up their pants and took off.

I pointed this out to one of our people standing next to me and said to him, "Let's do the same. If you'd like to come with me, I'll wait for you in the field behind the barn."

"OK," he said. "Let's go!"

I walked over to the guard and told him that I had to urinate. "Do it here, by the side of the road," he said to me.

"How can I?" I replied "There are women present. Let me go behind the barn instead. I'm leaving my belongings here, so you can be sure I won't run away." I left the few pieces of underwear I was carrying, which were all the worldly possessions I could call my own.

The soldier was watching me, but then he turned away, and I ran into the field, lay down in the grass, and waited for the other fellow. He came over a few minutes later, and we took off together.

We soon encountered a few Austrians along the way, who told us to come with them. "This time," they told us, "we won't get caught. There are only a few of us, and we'll wait until it gets dark. Then we'll cross the border and go to Linz."

It was a hard decision to make. I wanted to get away from the Russians, but at the same time I was thinking of the other groups coming from Vienna and walking right into the arms of the border guards. We thanked them and started to walk back and to look for a railroad station.

We walked toward the Danube and then along the river until we found a spot where small rowboats were ferrying people to the other side. It took us a couple of hours, but we eventually located a station in Saint Valentin. We hit the jackpot. A four-car passenger train was being assembled to leave for Vienna. One of the cars had a big sign that read: Nur für K-zetler (for concentration camp inmates only). At the car door stood a man who said "Amchu," to which we answered "Amchu" and were let in. We found a few Jews inside who told us that they'd given a bottle of vodka to the Russian stationmaster, and he'd given them the car.

We passed many bombed-out railroad stations. One of the most unforgettable sights I saw was Saint Polten, where completely destroyed trains had been pushed aside and piled one on top of the other, rails pointing into the sky as if bent by giants' hands. Some of the stations had been completely destroyed, with little signs telling us the names of the places.

We pulled into the Westbahnhof station at midnight and were able to stop a group from leaving for the border. After spending the night at the station, we returned to the school at Slaghoffgasse.

Later in the day, Yuri Wenglishevsky, the leader of the Vienna Brichah, came over to have a talk with us. After we told him what had happened to us, he said, "I am proud of you, and of your way of thinking, and I will be very happy to take you into our Brichah. We need men like you who think about others more than about themselves."

We gladly accepted his invitation and were taken to Frankgasse, Vienna, where the headquarters of the Brichah was located. A new page in my life was being written. I was becoming a Brichahnik.

CHAPTER 8

LIFE IN THE BRICHAH

A big surprise awaited me when I arrived at Frankgasse. Sara and Tusia, the two girls from my hometown, and Yojnale, my new friend, were also working for the Brichah. Chanina (the man who'd fallen off the train in Romania) and his wife were there, too. I also met the man who wasn't there: Robert, who was to meet us in Mauthausen, came back to Vienna. He'd waited the whole week for a transport, but none came. With all the telephone lines down, he'd had no way of finding out what was happening, so he'd decided to return home.

"Mauthausen is out," said Jury, our leader. "We must find a new crossing to get our transports to the American zone. If Vienna gets overcrowded, then the whole forward movement from the east will stop, and nobody would be able to get out from Poland, Czechoslovakia, Hungary, or Romania. So let's go to it!"

Now the preparations for our mission began. Sitting around a table with a large map of Austria, we searched for the most likely crossing along the Russian-American demarcation line. The border ran along the River Enns and across the Danube, and then it was a land border all the way to the Czechoslovakian border. The River Enns looked like our best option, so we decided to go there and have a look at the territory.

Chanina, Shlamek, Chanale, Moniek, Anshel, and I were the first to go. The trip from Vienna to Saint Valentin was uneventful. We arrived at noon and walked to the River Enn, which had two bridges, both of which were blocked with barbed wire and were watched by Russian border police.

They yelled at us, "*Davay nazad!* ["Go back!"] You can't come near the border!"

We withdrew and sat down in a field to make alternate plans. We decided to split up into two groups: Moniek, Chanale, and Anshel went north toward the Danube, while Chanina, Shlamek, and I went back to Saint Valentin to take a shuttle to Steyr.

The town of Steyr was divided by the river, with one side belonging to the Russians and the other to the Americans. We left the train at the station and walked along the railroad tracks until we came to a bridge. This bridge was also barricaded, with Russians standing on it so that they would have a better view of the river. A highway ran alongside the river, so we took this road. The Russians could see every move we made, and we had to walk a few miles until we came to a sharp bend in the river. Then we decided to investigate this section.

We found an abandoned farmhouse and made it our shelter for the night. Our food supplies consisted of the few slices of salted pork and black bread the transports had brought to Vienna from Budapest. Vienna did not have any food, and Hungary was our only food source.

The night was warm, which we were thankful for, because the house had no roof. In the morning, after a breakfast of dry bread and cold water from the well, we went to work.

We found out that a few farmers along the river had boats, which we would be able to use to cross the river. Much to our dismay, however, we found out that the Russians had machine-gunned the boats full of holes. Going from farmer to farmer, we eventually found one who'd hidden a few rubber pontoons and was willing to move our transports across the river for one dollar per person.

Having made the deal, we then started back to Vienna. This time we avoided the highway, since we were trying to find a safer way across for larger transports. We took the scenic route, over fields, woods, hills, and gullies. It was a difficult trip, and we worried if older people and women with children would be able to make it. We were sure they would make it somehow. They had escaped Siberia, the partisans, and the concentration camps, so this would be child's play to them.

Back in Steyr, we heard that the Americans would be taking over the whole town and the surrounding territory. We could not depend on rumors, though, so we decided to proceed with our plans.

We made it to Vienna, where I learned the news that the whole group who'd been caught while crossing the border with me had returned from Mauthausen. The Russians had kept them in a camp for a couple of days and, after checking their identities and confiscating a few watches, they let them go with a warning not to ever try to illegally make their way across the border again. Some of the Germans among them were arrested on suspicion of being SS men.

The northern group came back without finding anything: too many Russian patrols along the way.

The new route was to go through Steyr. I was elected to take the first group of forty boys and girls for a test run. I also had with me six boys who would be the future transport leaders.

We left Vienna at midnight and twelve hours later arrived in Saint Valentin. The shuttle was ready to leave, and half an hour later, we were in Steyr. The same farmhouse we'd used on our exploration trip now became our resting place for the night.

In the morning, "Operation Breakthrough" started.

Not wanting to take the road, we climbed the hills and crossed brooks until we made it to the river and the pontoons. A few trips later and forty dollars lighter and they were all safely on the other side.

Five of the six helpers refused to come back and stayed on the American side. Only Heniek, whom I briefly mentioned earlier in connection with nearly getting separated from his wife by the Gestapo, was willing to come back with me.

A surprise awaited us when we got to the railroad station. The place was empty, and the gates were locked. Not a living soul in sight. We had nowhere to go, so we climbed over the fence and sat down to eat. It looked like the rumors about the Russians leaving and the Americans taking over were true after all. We now had to cross a new border that hadn't been there yesterday.

We suddenly heard the sound of a locomotive, and a few minutes later a train hauling old rickety boxcars pulled into the station. A few Russian soldiers picked up anything on wheels and hauled it away.

We walked over to the soldiers and asked if they would take us with them. They looked at us as if we were crazy. One of the soldiers asked, "Why would you want to come with us? The Americans are coming here, and they have good food, cigarettes, and candy. You'd have to be stupid to leave."

I told him that we didn't want to live among the capitalists and that we wanted to go back to Poland, where our help was needed to start to rebuild the country. Laughing, they allowed us to board the train. In Saint Valentin, we got on a train back to Vienna. From the train, we could see the Americans moving into Vienna. Vienna, until this point under Russian occupation, was now divided into four zones. We were lucky to find ourselves in the American zone, but we had to sit down and make new plans.

"Let's try Steyr again," someone suggested. "It's now a dry border."

We had nothing to lose, and we had to get our people out of Vienna. Our transit camp was getting overcrowded, so we had to acquire another camp. The old place was now in the French zone, and we were given the Westminster Hotel as our new transit camp, which was located in the American zone.

CHAPTER 9

THE SECOND TRY

I was again sent to Saint Valentin, this time with two helpers as future transport leaders and a group of young boys and girls. We only took the shuttle as far as Solingen this time, where the Russians told us to keep away from the border.

An Austrian we met was willing to guide us across but insisted that we pay him in advance. The terrain was very bad—impossible for older people and children, he said—and too many Russians around. The high hills were threaded by steep, narrow paths. Sometimes we had to climb on all fours.

After a few hours of walking, we found ourselves alone, surrounded by Russians. Our guide had disappeared, and we suspected that this had been his plan from the beginning. We were taken to their command post, which was located in a Gasthaus.

I presented a letter from the Geneva Red Cross that stated, "To all military personnel! This is to certify that Mr. Saul Birnbaum is a transport leader whose job is to bring these refugees to the country of their origin. We would appreciate if you would give him any help he needs in performing his duty." It was written on Red Cross stationery, in both English and Russian. It looked very legitimate.

The officer read the document and said to me, "I will let you go to the Americans, if you let some of the girls come to a party we are having this evening; they will catch up with you in the morning." I could not agree to such a deal, so he told us to go back. Only one girl decided to stay, and nothing I said to her would change her mind. She was in a hurry to get across and did not care how she did it. I was afraid to force her to come with us, so as not to arouse suspicion.

The railroad station in Saint Valentin was constantly crowded with refugees trying to get to the American zone. Some of them told me that there were two crossings: Mauthausen and Urfahr. Mauthausen had a ferry that went across the Danube to the American zone, and farther north was the town of Urfahr, connected by a bridge to Linz. With a pass, one could go by trolley from one side to the other.

Saul Birnbaum

Back in Vienna, transports were still coming from the east and were being sent south to Graz in the British zone, but the main objective was to open the passage to the American zone.

Shlamek, Moniek, and I took a group to try the Linz-Urfahr crossing. The train took us to Saint Valentin, which was the last stop on the Russian side. Everybody had to get off and find other ways of transportation. As usual, the town was full of refugees looking for a way to get to the American side.

I met somebody at the station whom I was sure would be on the American side by now. It was the girl from our last transport who'd stayed with the Russians. She told me that she'd gone to the party and had had a good time, but the Russians sent her back the next morning, and she'd been wandering around since then. Luckily, the Russians hadn't asked her too many questions or else they would have found out about our transports. They were interested in something else. A steady stream of people was leaving town toward the Danube, and we joined them.

The road led downhill through narrow country roads, so the people spread out into the fields. Looking down from above, it looked like a horde of wildebeests on the move. The fields close to the river were trampled by the masses of refugees passing through there day after day.

For ten shillings, small boats ferried people across the Danube. When we reached Mauthausen, we found out that the ferry was out of order, so we had to hitchhike a ride to Urfahr. The town was also full of refugees trying to get across the river to Linz, but to be able to do that, a special two-way pass was required. The Burgermeister was giving these passes out, and we were able to secure four passes. The big question was how we would get twenty people across with only four passes. When we got to the bridge again, we were greeted by a big crowd. The whole of Austria was full of crowds, it seemed.

The trolley came, and everybody pushed to get a seat. The soldiers let in only as many people as could be seated. Three people from the transport and one of the leaders went, then half an hour later, he came back with the permits. The second group then went, and we kept going back and forth, until we were all safely in Linz.

A special ceremony was connected with the crossing from the Russian zone to the American zone. It involved a DDT dusting. The whole procedure went like this. You presented your permit to the Russian soldier, and he let you sit down on a seat in the trolley. When all the seats were occupied, the trolley traveled to the American side, where a second permit inspection took place, after which we had to line up for a shot of a miracle powder, DDT. American soldiers holding large hand pumps filled with a white powder were waiting for us. A few seconds later, we were covered from head to toe with that powder. They even gave us a few shots inside our shirts and pants. It was supposed to kill all the lice we'd no doubt picked up on the Russian side. Even if one stayed there for a few minutes, one had to undergo this ceremony. That day I received three dustings in the span of two hours.

It was late in the evening when we reached the transit camp, called Bindermichl. After a day's rest, the transport leaders went back to Vienna.

We used that way a few more times, with our boys from Linz waiting every day at the crossing for a transport. It was slow and tedious work that wasn't suitable for large transports.

And then came Mauthausen.

Not the Mauthausen where thousands of Jewish prisoners had been killed by the Nazis in the stone quarries, but a Mauthausen that we planned to make a gateway to freedom for our people.

The first large transport of a hundred people had made it without any difficulty, so we got ready for a big push. A list of two hundred names was made up, and I mean "made up": names like Moishe Zeechmich, Mode Ani, and other names we could think up. We used these same lists of names many times over, because we could rarely go to the authorities for new permits.

The first page, in German and English, gave us permission to transport the two hundred refugees whose names appeared on the following pages to the towns in the American, French, and British zones. The papers were signed by the American Military Command in Vienna.

The first group of men, women, and children was taken to the railroad station. We secured two cars and put up signs that read, "FOR CONCENTRATION CAMP INMATES ONLY!" No one dared enter the cars.

The trip to Saint Valentin was easy. We found a farmer who rented us a tractor and two trailers, which we loaded up with the bundles and the older people and children. Then we started out toward the Danube. The progress was slow, and the waiting for the boats was long. It was dark by the time we'd finished ferrying the people across. We had to stay overnight in a barn near the river. In the morning, after a five-mile walk, we arrived at Mauthausen.

I promised myself that after the job was finished, I would visit the stone quarry where so many of our people had been worked to death.

First, though, I had two hundred men, women, and children to get to the Americans. We approached the road leading to the ferry, where a soldier told me to get the OK from the commandant, whose office was across the street in a Gast Haus (inn). I introduced myself as the transport leader and presented my papers, the list of names, my ID from the Jewish Refugee Committee, or JRC—that was our official name—and a letter from the Geneva Red Cross. I also wore an armband with the Red Cross emblem on it. He was very impressed and started to question me. We spoke in Russian.

"What nationality are you?

"I am a Polish Jew. I signed up for one year with the Red Cross, after which I'll go back to my homeland."

We talked for a while, had a few vodkas, and then he accompanied me to the checkpoint and told the soldiers to let me pass. I went over with my people, showed the Americans our papers, and that was that. The job was done, and I was on the ferry and on my way back, knowing that a big new door had just opened in the wall surrounding Eastern Europe.

The stone quarry was silent and peaceful. I closed my eyes and tried to envision the horrible scenes that had occurred here just a few months before. In my mind I could hear the screams of people being crushed by the large stones they had to carry on their backs from the bottom of the quarry. That was the only time I ever went there. Too much pain.

Shlamek, Moniek, and I worked there until December 1945, when the train started to go across the bridge into the American zone. We took three transports every week. Each transport had two hundred people, and it worked like clockwork, so it turned into a routine job after a while.

I took a transport to Saint Valentin, where one of the other transport leaders was back from his job. He gave me the permit and his shoes. They weren't his shoes, but our shoes, the only good pair that fit all three of us. They came in handy, especially in bad weather when we had to walk through the fields with the mud reaching our ankles. The mud was so thick that I had to use my hands to help pull my feet from that dough, kneaded by hundreds of feet.

Every good thing has to end, so this, too, ended.

To whom do you think it happened? It happened on my trip.

The whole trip was going fine. The Russians let us on the ferry, and we arrived at the American side. They checked our papers, counted the people, and let us pass. Everything was in order, so I gave my two helpers the final instructions and had started for the ferry when I heard someone calling my name. I turned around and saw that the whole group had been stopped at the second barrier.

When I came over, I was told that my permit was invalid, because an Allied Commission was now in control of Vienna, and all permits had to have been issued by the commission in four languages. I would have to go back to Vienna and get the proper papers.

My pleas to let the transport pass fell on deaf ears. I tried to explain to them that we had no food or money for the train, but it did not help. Then I said, "We are not going back! My people are afraid that the Russians will put them in jail." I was really afraid. We had a Russian major and his family and two lieutenants, all Jewish. They had guns and were ready to kill themselves if they were forced to go back. (I hadn't been told about them when we'd left Vienna.) There was no way the Americans could make us go back. They were not SS men, after all, and they would not shoot us.

The Americans told me that I would have to go to their command post and talk it over with their commander. They put me in a jeep for the trip; the post was a few miles away. Before I left, I said to the group, "Run in different directions and try to get to Bindermichl. There are only a few soldiers here. So when I come back, I hope you'll be gone."

My mission was unsuccessful. The major kept insisting, "We have orders from Vienna not to let anybody into our zone without a permit from them."

At that time, my English was very limited, but I tried to the best of my ability to get him to understand my predicament. "Please," I said, "I have my orders to take these people to a camp in Linz. They are tired and hungry, and a trip back would be very hard for them. It is also possible that the Russians will put them in a camp, and many of them would die." Nothing helped.

I was put on a truck with twenty soldiers in full battle dress, with guns, ammo belts, and helmets, and we returned to the border.

The people did what I had told them to do. Only sixty-eight of them remained, mostly old people and families with small children. The soldiers surrounded them, but we still refused to go.

The officer started to shout at us. The women started to cry and call them SS men. That, too, did not help. It was a picture of days gone by not so long ago. The only difference was that we answered them back without fear of a bullet.

After a while, the officer came over to me and said, "I'll come across with you and your people and explain the problem to the Russians."

We couldn't hold out much longer. The people were frightened, hungry, and tired, and it was getting late. We walked to the ferry and went back. The American came with us. He did not speak Russian, so I told them that the Americans wanted the papers signed by the Russian authorities. (I did not tell them the part about me having to go back to Vienna to get a permit.) The presence of the American seems to have convinced the Russians that I was telling the truth.

We were permitted to get off the ferry. I was told to go to their headquarters in a town ten kilometers away and to get the papers signed.

First I settled my people in the Red Cross shelter. Then I took a man with me and went to get the signature. We found the place without any trouble. We were brought to the commandant's room and were told to wait. A few minutes later, a gray-haired captain came in, his chest full of medals. He sat down and asked how he could help me.

I got up and said, "Tovarish Kapitan (comrade captain). I am with the Geneva Red Cross and am a transport leader. I have two hundred people who've spent many years in concentration camps and now are on their way home. Your soldiers were very helpful to me, but the Americans gave me a hard time. I would like to get them on their way as soon as possible. The only thing we need is your permission and signature on this list."

He took my papers, looked them over, and told his secretary to type in the back in Russian, "I give permission to the people listed on the other pages to return to their homes, and order all the military and civilian authorities to give them all the necessary help they need." It had his signature and two red stamps. We used that paper for a very long time.

After our return, I took twenty people to the ferry. The captain looked at the signature, and I told him that I had to send the twenty people across, because I had no place for them to stay. The others were spread out among the surrounding farms, and it would take me a while to round them all up.

He called me by my Russian name and said, "It's OK, Sasha!" To the soldier he said, "Mark down the twenty who are going now, and make sure that no more than two hundred pass."

They made it without any difficulty. I returned and took another ten. They, too, were let go by the Amis, but this was all it would be for that evening, since the ferry did not operate after dark.

In the morning, two more groups of ten each went across without any papers; I stayed on the ferry, not wanting to show myself to the Americans. Only eighteen were left now, and I was thinking the ordeal would soon be over, but here again my bad luck intervened. The Russian let them pass, just adding eighteen to the number of people who'd gone through. I was watching from the Russian side. I saw them get off the ferry and walk up from the river to the checkpoint. I was ready to walk away when I saw one of the men waving his arm, indicating for me to come over.

An American soldier who'd been on duty the previous day recognized one of the men and had asked for the papers. I had to come over and show them to him. The soldier didn't know exactly what it was all about, so I told him to call the commandant and ask him if it was OK to let us pass with the papers they'd requested yesterday. He was told to let us go.

We put those papers in plastic and got out a few more transports of them. More and more people were arriving in Vienna at that time, and we needed more room. In October 1945, the Americans handed over the Rothschild Hospital to the Brichah.

The transports came from Budapest and Bratislava to Vienna. From there, the transports were sent to Linz, and from there to Salzburg. Salzburg was near the German border, where the majority of transports were being shipped. A great number of displaced persons (DP) camps had to be filled, and the people could stay in Germany until they were sent on their way to Israel. Smaller groups were sent to Innsbruck, and from there through the Brenner Pass to the Italian seaports and then by boat to Israel.

CHAPTER 10

VIENNA

*G*emütlichkeit (relaxation) was something I heard a lot of but had no time to enjoy. I was always busy, either coming back from a transport or getting ready for the next one. The time eventually came when we could slow down. Our staff got larger, and we were able to take it easy. Each of us took a transport once a week, which meant that we were away two or three days and could use the other days to get a little of that Gemütlichkeit.

Vienna was beautiful, despite a few bombed-out neighborhoods, and I fell in love with the city: the coffeehouses, restaurants, *Weinkellers* (wine cellars), and *Weingartens* (wine gardens) serving the *Heurigen (wine of the day)*. There wasn't much food around at the time, but if you brought your own, they would supply the service and the wine. Our tables would often be the only one set with food at a restaurant; the natives drank wine and peeked longingly at our feast, but we didn't give a damn. They'd had their seven good years while we went hungry, and now the wheel of fortune had turned our way.

Food wasn't the only thing we were interested in. We were getting some culture too: we saw the Hoffburg, the Habsburg palace, which consisted of hundreds of rooms, only a few of which were open. The palace's treasures were boxed up and hidden in the cellars, so we had to believe what the guides told us about them, and we hoped one day to come back and see the palace in all its splendor. We saw the Spanish Riding School with the white Lippizaner horses, museums, Saint Stephan's Cathedral, and the Prater. Not everything was operating, but it was still interesting. We visited the Grinzing, the Wienerwald, the Schönbrunn Palace, and much more.

Our apartment on Frankgasse was getting overcrowded, because our family was getting larger all the time. Some of our young people were falling in love and getting married. Messengers and *chayalim* (Israeli soldiers) from all over Europe passed through. The apartment had many rooms full of antique furniture and mementoes of times past. The former owner was a doctor, a Nazi and a personal friend of Adolph Hitler. The place was filled with photos and letters signed by Hitler and lots of Nazi medals. We were young and stupid and destroyed everything—even the furniture, which we used for firewood. This was one way we could take revenge on the Nazis.

Every time we went with a transport, we left the Gemütlichkeit behind us. Every trip to Mauthausen was a new adventure. There was always a new problem that had never happened before. Once we arrived late in the evening and went straight to the Red Cross shelter. The people working there made supper for us. They were always ready to help us out. And why not? We supplied them with American cigarettes and soap.

Around midnight, some loud hammering at the door woke us up. Three Russian soldiers came in and demanded that we send a few girls to clean their headquarters. "It's now after midnight," I said. "Tomorrow morning I'll be glad to give you as many people as you need, but I won't permit you to take anybody tonight!" They left without the girls. They knew me, because they'd seen me many times drinking vodka with their commandant.

In the morning, when I went to the ferry to send my people across, the commandant called me into his office and told me that he was angry for what I'd done last night.

"We always get a few refugees from the shelter to clean our offices at night," he said. "During the day, it's impossible to do anything here. Too many people around."

"I'm really sorry," I said. "We've never been here at night, and I was afraid to let the soldiers take the girls away. If you'd been there, I would have been glad to send them over."

"*Khorosho*, Sasha! But next time, better not refuse my men anything, or the border will be closed for you!"

Sometimes funny things happened to us, like the deals people made on the ferry, which was a kind of no-man's-land. The Americans and the Russians were permitted to ride the ferry from one side to the other, but they could not leave the ferry. So this became the marketplace, where all transactions took place. The hottest items on the market were still wrist watches. I remembered back in 1939, when the Russians had come into our town and bought up all the watches. Now, six years later, they were still buying them. One time I watched two soldiers conducting business. The American had two watches for sale, and the Russian had a handful of twenty-dollar bills. The exchange took place. The two watches that could have been bought in the PX (for "post exchange," or commissary) for a few dollars sold for a hundred.

When we landed on the Russian side, I heard the Russian soldier tell his friends that he'd bought the two watches from the stupid American using old money. The soldier had probably confiscated that money from some poor refugee.

We encountered a lot problems with our people. One time, the train was stopped at the station in Saint Pölten for a spot check, which was the worst thing that could've happened. These checks sometimes took hours before the whole train was inspected. There was always the chance that one of the children who'd been born in Russia would say something to the soldiers. Our permits stated that these were Austrian or Greek refugees who were not supposed to know Russian, but sometimes a young boy or girl would ask a soldier for water. Sometimes I had to slap people to make them obey my orders. It was nerve-racking for me, especially when the soldiers saw so many young girls among us.

I remember on one transport, we could only get boxcars—nothing else was available. As usual, we stopped in Saint Pölten. It was late at night and, as usual, the soldiers came out to see the girls. I told my people to sit tight, but one of the girls had to go out. She went up to the caboose on top of a car. I saw the girl walk up but was too late to stop her. A soldier was already on his way toward the caboose. I rushed over to cut him off. He stopped, looked at me, and said, "You better leave me be. I just want to have a good time. I won't harm her."

"You can't have her!" I said. "Don't you know that all the people in this transport were in concentration camps and that the Germans performed experiments on them? She could have syphilis or some other disease."

He took out a small box from his pocket and said, "I don't have to worry about that. I have sulfadin pills." By that time the girl had come down, so I took her with me back to the car.

CHAPTER 11

THE TELEGRAM

One afternoon we were sending off a transport from the Südbahnhof to Graz. It was not my job to do so, but when we were in Vienna, we helped the others. Yuri, the leader of the Vienna Brichah I mentioned earlier, came over and handed me a valise with food and some pengö, the Hungarian monetary unit. He told me that we had to send a telegram to Budapest, but we couldn't send it from Austria. I'd have to take a train to the border, cross into any town in Hungary, and send the telegram from there. He gave me the message, written in Hungarian, and told me to copy it on a telegram form and then make my way back to Vienna.

The train was full of Russians. I sat down next to a lieutenant, and after a while we started to converse.

He told me about his home and how happy he was to go back to his *kolchoz* (collective farm) near Kiev. I told him how I'd survived the concentration camps and that I was going back to Budapest, after bringing a transport to Vienna.

It was getting dark when we heard a tremendous explosion. The train stopped, and after waiting for over an hour, we were told that the tracks ahead were ripped up and that the train would not proceed any farther. The conductor told us that we would have to walk about ten miles to the border. We left our train and could see the flashes and hear explosions in the distance. After it quieted down, we started to walk until we passed the place where the explosion had occurred. A train was derailed and blown to bits. The soldiers suspected sabotage from the Nazis or the anti-communists.

We came to a small station after a while, where the Russians appropriated a locomotive and two boxcars. The stationmaster refused to give them to the soldiers until they threatened him with a gun. We all piled in, and the train left. After we crossed the border but before the train pulled into the station, it slowed down, which gave me a chance to jump off and sneak into town without passing a border check.

It was still dark, and I hid in a doorway till daylight; when people started to walk around in the streets, I left my hideout and found a post office.

Mission accomplished, I ate breakfast and made my way to the Jewish Committee to get help for my return to Vienna. "No!" was their answer. "We can't get you across. Who are you? And what are you doing here?" I presented my credentials and told them that I'd brought a transport from Austria and now was having trouble getting back.

They told me that no trains were running and that I had to find my own way back. One of the men told me to buy two bottles of vodka and go to the border checkpoint, which was located on the outskirts of town. He said the border police were stopping all the trucks and that I could get a driver to take me with him in exchange for a bottle of vodka.

The aroma of wine permeated the air. It was the time of wine making, and the streets were full of carts laden with squeezed-out grapes. The smell was strong enough to get you drunk. The fruit stands were loaded with fruits we couldn't even dream about in Vienna. I bought as much fruit as I could carry and two bottles of vodka.

At the checkpoint, I presented my papers to the Russians and told them the same story I'd told the people at the Jewish Committee. A woman soldier who could read English told the others that the papers were from the Geneva Red Cross and that I should be sent back on the first truck that came along. Several Russian soldiers were waiting for transportation, but I was the first to get a seat. About two hours later, I stepped down from the army truck in front of our headquarters in Frankgasse. The driver had delivered me at my doorstep in exchange for the vodka.

The border bridge across the River Enns was reopened in the middle of November, and our job became much easier. No more miles of walking from the railroad station to the border. After a check of documents, the train would proceed to the American side.

With the transports going directly to Linz, life became easy in Vienna. We had more help and we went to the border once a week, so we had more time to relax and enjoy ourselves. The city was starting to return to normalcy. Theaters and restaurants were reopening all over town, and we used this occasion to soak in a little culture.

More and more people were leaving Poland, and the Rothschild Hospital was always full. We now sent transports of two to three hundred people to Linz. Bindermichl in that city was a development in which German officers and their families had lived during the glorious days of the Third Reich. Now, the officers were still there, doing manual labor. As prisoners of war, they kept this DP camp clean, coming in under guard every morning and returning to their camp every evening.

Several Jewish families lived there permanently; each family had a nice apartment. We also had a transit camp where our transports stopped on their way to Salzburg. Many of our boys now worked at different points to keep the transports going without a stop. Transit camps were now open in Steyr, Wells, and Bad Hall.

One time, I was leading a transport to Linz. The train stopped at the bridge over the Enns for inspection. The Russians were entering one car at a time, inspecting papers. When they came to my car, I walked out and saw my friend, the commandant from the Mauthausen border point. After a friendly greeting, he asked me if I still worked for the Red Cross. I told him that I had two cars filled with refugees. He asked if my papers were in order, and I said to him, "Yes, you know me, I'm always legitimate."

"OK. You can keep your people inside," he said. To the soldiers he said, "Leave the two last cars alone. Sasha said that everything's in order." It was good to have friends in high places in my line of work.

It was easier to get along with the Russians than with the Americans. Normally, we did send a transport by train to the American zone, where our people from Linz took over. But once in a while, the Americans would try to send a transport back to the Russian side. Our people had a standing order that if something like that ever happened, the whole transport should get off the train, sit down on the ground, and under no circumstances return to the Russian zone.

One day our worst fears did come true. A transport of 250 people passed the Russian zone without any problems but was stopped by the Americans, who wanted the whole transport returned to Vienna. The people from the transport left the train, sat down on the ground, and declared a sit-down strike. The Americans used force, but our people refused to budge. They were eventually sent to a DP camp in Enns, not far from Linz.

The month of October was like any other month, rainy and cool, but for me it was like spring. I fell in love. Until now I'd gone out with a few girls, but never anything serious. One day, a woman named Rutka came to Frankgasse, and as soon as I saw her, I knew she was the one. We saw each other every day, and I felt very bad when she went home for the night.

Time was now passing fast. I made contact with my family in America through a soldier I'd met. He told me that he was going back home to New York, so I gave him the address of my uncle, never expecting that he would actually take the time to look them up. But he did. One day I received a package from them, through an organization. The contents were unusable—it was cocoa mixed with Diamond Kosher salt—but despite that, I was happy. I was not alone.

In a letter that followed, I found out that my uncle Isaak (my mother's brother) and his family, as well as my uncles Joe and Sam (my father's two brothers) and their families, all lived in New York. Since that time, I started to dream about going to America. My grandmother also lived there. She was still alive and hoped to be able to see me. They wrote that they were rushing an affidavit with the hope that I would be in America while Grandma was still alive.

I wrote them that I'd met a girl and that the only way I could come to America would be with Rutka as my wife. All that took time. By the end of November, Rutka received news that her sister was alive in Germany, so she decided to go there to see her. No matter how much I implored her, she refused to change her mind. I took her with a transport to Linz, where I said a tearful goodbye to Rutka. That was the last time I saw her. Somehow, I came back to Vienna. Somehow, I passed the days as if in a fog. My friends started to worry about me. My moping got so bad that they soon decided to send me on a vacation.

CHAPTER 12

MY VACATION

"Two weeks in Paris will surely make you forget your lost love," they said, and preparations began. The easiest way to travel would be as a chayal, so our tailor made a soldier's uniform for me, and our document maker prepared all the necessary documents, including a soldier's passport with my name and photo. We had plenty of blanks, so the document maker used a hard-boiled egg to transfer the stamp from a soldier's book to the one I was going to use. No kidding. He took a hard-boiled egg, peeled and still hot, and rolled it over the stamped page and then pressed it on the proper spot on the blank book. It was hard to tell the difference.

Everything was ready, but at the last minute I changed my mind. Instead of going to Paris, I decided to go back once more to Poland, with the hope of finding my younger brother.

Chanina obtained a transit pass from the Czechoslovakian embassy, permitting me to enter their country from Hungary and leave at the Polish border. The boys scraped together some pengö for spending money in Budapest. On the fifteenth of December, I left Vienna in the company of Helen, a messenger from Germany who was going to Budapest and then on to Bucharest.

What a change I saw in Budapest. The prices were sky-high. The inflation reminded me of the stories my father told me about the German mark during World War I. The banknotes had been printed in thousand- and million-mark denominations. I couldn't understand it the time, but in Budapest, in December 1945, I saw how it worked.

A bottle of beer I'd bought in June for twenty-five pengö now sold for 350. The money I paid for a two-page newspaper weighed more than the paper itself. The conductor in the trolley didn't even count the money; he just dumped it into a paper bag that stood on the floor. All the coins my friends had given me in Vienna amounted to nothing. A pack of very bad cigarettes that sold in the morning for one thousand pengö cost fifteen hundred pengö by the afternoon. A dinner in a restaurant could be had for five thousand to ten thousand pengö, which was too steep for our pockets, so a piece of speck and some black bread kept us going during our stay in Budapest.

I had one pound of American coffee and one pound of tea with me, which I planned to bring to my friends in Poland. Everybody told me to sell it, because it would be confiscated at one of the borders. I went down to a grocery store and was offered a million pengö for it. Even in one-thousand-pengö denominations, it was a sizable pile of paper, too much to carry with me. It was worth about two dollars, so I decided to take a chance and bring the coffee and tea with me.

I left Budapest for Bratislava and two days later was nearing the Polish border. During the trip, I became friendly with a Russian officer who was traveling in the same direction as I. He was with a group of soldiers but had become separated from them. I had a small rucksack with my possessions, and he had a large bag with food for the whole group. We switched. I gave him my small pack and took the large one from him; this way, I could be sure that the coffee, tea, and the letters my friends gave me to take to Poland would be safe. Nobody dared search the Russian, while I was checked a few times, even though my documents were in order in Czechoslovakia.

The train pulled into *Zebrzydowice*, the last station on the Czech side. The station building was divided into two parts: one for soldiers, and the other for civilians. Being with the Russian, I sat in their waiting room; when the train came, he told me to follow him. This was my undoing.

The other waiting room had a ticket window at which civilians bought their tickets. I didn't see it and thus didn't pay my fare. We walked out to the other side of the building and were now in Poland. A shuttle train was waiting there, and we boarded it for a short ride to Dziedzice, the first Polish town.

As soon as we left the station, the Polish conductor demanded my ticket, which I did not have. He asked for my documents, and the Russian told him to let me be, because he'd traveled with me from Hungary and knew that my papers were in order. A quarrel started, and the conductor asked me again for my entry papers. I did not have any.

The correct procedure would have been to go to the Polish Repatriation Committee and get myself repatriated to Poland. The only paper I had was a Brichah parole, which was good at any of our stations all over Europe. It was a small square of paper written in Hebrew, and it would get me help in any city in any country in which the Brichah was active. I knew that it would not help me in this situation, though.

The Russian tried again to convince the conductor that everything was in order, but he was told to shut up or he would be put under arrest. That's when the officer called it quits. He gave me back my rucksack, grabbed his bag, and moved to the next compartment.

When the train stopped at the station, the conductor handed me over to a Polish militiaman, who led me away to the police station and handed me over to a lieutenant for interrogation. The police station was located in a private villa, and the large living room had been converted into an office. My rucksack was taken from me and the contents scattered on the piano.

I was asked if these were my belongings, and when I said yes, he looked them over. He pushed aside my underwear, looked at the coffee and tea, and then found the letters. He started to read—the letters were written in Polish—looked at me, and smiled. "My, my," he said. "So we've got ourselves a real-life smuggler! We're looking for guys like you who are smuggling people out of Poland."

"What are you talking about?" I asked.

He pushed the letters in my face. "Read it and tell me what it says!"

I took one letter and started to read.

Dear Nusiek,

I am now in Vienna. My trip was OK. It's very easy if you go with a group from the Brichah. Ask Siolek [that's my Polish name], and he'll put you in touch with the proper people.

Love, Mandek

Mandek was an old friend of mine. That was enough. I didn't have to read anymore. I realized how stupid it had been of me not to have read the letters before I took them with me.

"Sir!" I said. "Please let me go. You can keep the tea and coffee. I also have an Italian pocket watch, which you may keep. What good will it do me if the NKVD takes me away?"

He didn't answer but called a militiaman and told him to lock me up. The militiaman pushed me into a room and closed the door. I found myself in an already-occupied bathroom. The man asked me why I was there.

"No papers. And you?"

"Well, with me, it's just the opposite. I had too many papers."

He told me that he lived in Munich and had bought two birth certificates for his brother and sister so that they could be repatriated as German citizens. He'd been waiting for a train when the militia made a spot check and found the papers.

I said, "I offered the lieutenant a few things to let me go; I hope he'll take them."

"OK," he said. "If we get out of here, I'll pay you back half your losses."

I spent the night on the toilet seat, my cellmate in the bathtub. They didn't give us any food that evening, and I hadn't eaten anything since noon. In the morning, when the lieutenant came in to shave, I repeated my offer. He walked out without saying a word.

We were given black bread and coffee for breakfast. Then they took me to see the lieutenant. My papers were still on the piano, but the coffee, tea, and the watch were gone. He ordered me to pack my belongings and said, "If I let you go, will you promise me never to show your face here ever again?"

"Yes, sir!" I said. They took me back to the bathroom and took the other fellow out. He came back about ten minutes later, and a militiaman escorted us to the railroad station and put us on a train to Katowice. When I asked the other guy for some money, he told me that they'd taken away all his money, too.

When I got to Katowice, I went to a bakery at an address I was given in Vienna. After showing my parole paper, I was taken to a Brichah safe house. I was told to stay there for a few days until new identification papers could be made up for me. They gave me a few zlotys and sent me on my way to Lodz.

At the station, as I was waiting in line for my ticket, I had a little adventure. Someone hit me over my head and threw down my Tyrolean hat. I looked around, thinking it was somebody I knew, but the man was screaming at the top of his voice, "I thought we got rid of all the Germans, and here we've got another one!" It took me some time to explain to him that I'd just come back from Austria and that I was Polish. Only then did he leave me alone. I didn't wear that hat again during my stay in Poland. My getup was kind of strange for that country: high Hungarian laced boots, riding britches, an Austrian hunter's coat with a fur collar, and a Tyrolean hat. Nobody paid attention to me in Vienna, but here, everybody turned to look at me.

The first thing I did when I arrived at the kibbutz in Lodz was to get some local clothing so that I wouldn't draw any more attention to myself. I stayed for two days at the kibbutz, where I was a VIP to the kids who were getting ready for the trip to Vienna. They kept me up all night, listening to the stories of my exploits, but I was impatient to see my hometown again.

I had a surprise when I came to deliver the letter—the one that had almost landed me in trouble—to Mandek's family. I handed the letter to his older brother, and he read it and started to laugh. I couldn't remember that there was anything to laugh about in the letter, but I, too, started to chuckle when he took me to the other room and I saw Mandek sleeping in the bed. He'd come back before me.

After checking the lists of the returned Jews and not finding any of the names of my relatives, I went to visit some of my friends. They were all interested in finding a way to get out, so I gave them all the information I could.

Two days in Przemysl was all I could take. Coming as I was from the American zone of Austria and enjoying the freedom we enjoyed there, I couldn't get used to the constant police checks in the streets.

What a disappointment!

Life in Przemysl was bleak for the Jews. The few who did not leave lived in constant danger to their lives. Nothing had changed. The AK and the Banderowcy (the Polish underground and the Ukrainian Nazi collaborators I mentioned earlier) were still fighting each other, but that did not stop them from robbing and killing Jews.

The weather was also bad. It was snowing, and the streets were slushy. With nothing else to expect and dangers lurking in the streets, I decided to go back to my new home in Vienna.

After visiting my father's grave and saying good-bye to my friends, I took a train to Katowice, leaving the town I was born in. I was sure that this would be the last time I would see Przemysl and Poland. I'd had enough of my good friends, the Poles and Ukrainians. With friends like that, who needs enemies?

It was Christmas Eve, a time of joy and good-will toward all men. The only joy I felt was from the knowledge that soon I would be out of that accursed country. Somehow, there was no goodwill in me toward the people around me. And there were plenty of people around me. The train was crowded, and there was no room inside the cars; many of the passengers had to stand on the walkways between the cars. A wet snow was coming down, and I stood outside, covered with a blanket, shivering and wet.

When I arrived at the Brichah office in Katowice, I discovered that I once again needed new papers. My back pants pocket had been cut open and my papers gone. Also my valise had been stolen. My permit to travel in Czechoslovakia was also gone. I was lucky that I'd hidden my parole papers in my clothing, or I would have been in real trouble.

I had a couple of days of rest, during which I occupied my time by burning Russian documents, medals, and army books that were taken away from people who passed through this point on their way west.

This time I was traveling as one of the people, and not as a transport leader. It felt strange. I often wanted to give advice but had to remind myself that this wasn't my border and that I was only there for the ride.

We spent New Year's Eve in an empty shed in the no-man's-land between the Polish and Czech borders. I was with a group of young boys and girls I'd met in Lodz. The border police spent the night celebrating, with our people supplying the vodka, and in the morning, nobody paid attention to us when we crossed into Czechoslovakia.

On January 1, 1946, we arrived in Prague. I was very sorry not to be able to see the famous old city. I was eager to get back to Vienna. After a restful night and a good breakfast, I left for the station to get a train for Bratislava.

When I arrived there, a surprise was awaiting me. Helen, the messenger who'd traveled with me two weeks before, was also there, waiting for the car from Vienna. The car came and took us back the same day. One hour later, the skyline of Vienna came into view. Back home again! That was the feeling I now had for that beautiful city.

As I stepped into the elevator, I could hear the sound of dance music. The apartment was full of people, and the tables were covered with white linen and loaded with all kinds of food. I was very surprised by such a welcome. I did not feel that important.

It was not for me, though: Antek, one of our boys, and a Hungarian girl named Esti were getting married. I never expected that this would happen so fast. Sometime in November, a chayal had come to Vienna with Esti. The soldier had brought her from Hungary with the idea of taking her to Israel to marry her, but Antek took her away from him. They even fought at one point, and the chayal almost shot

Antek. Looks like Antek was the winner in the end, though, since he was the one who was getting married. A few other weddings took place in Frankgasse in 1945: Heniek and Henia, Bolek and Greta, and Robert and Tusia. The boys and girls were lonely without their families, so they were getting married.

In Vienna, everything was moving fine. It was wintertime now, and our transports were in full swing, going by train and truck.

And then everything stopped.

The border at Salzburg was closed. They needed help, so they sent for specialists. Three old smugglers were selected: Antek, Yojnale, and me, Siolek. We would go there and open that door into Germany. We packed our things, which didn't take long, because we had few possessions. We took the next transport to Salzburg. The train passed through the border without any problems. I became very friendly with a Hungarian girl by the name of Eva whom I met on the trip. She was traveling with her older sister and brother and told them that she would stay with me in Salzburg, even if they went on to Germany.

And so a new chapter of my life started. A new place, and a new girl.

CHAPTER 13

SALZBURG

We arrived at Salzburg and were taken to camp Mülln VI. This was a transit camp, but for us it became a permanent home for a long time.

Salzburg was a very important Brichah point because of its size and its close proximity to the German border. Our transports went from Vienna to Salzburg and from there across the border to Ainring in Germany. The Brichah had other transit camps in Austria, but it used them only when camp Mülln was filled to capacity.

The camp was located at Augustiner Gasse no. 4, where the Augustin monks had a Biergarten. The building consisted of three large rooms, many smaller rooms, and a beer garden where people came to have a good time. The back of the building was in ruins, probably hit by an Allied bomb. In 1945 it was turned into a transit camp for the Brichah. The large rooms were used as sleeping quarters for the refugees, while the smaller ones were made into living facilities for the workers.

At another camp, called Parsh, whole families of refugees lived in houses that had been previously occupied by the SS. Later the Jews enlarged the camp by building bungalow-type homes, which they took with them when they immigrated to Israel. The United Nations Refugee Organization (UNRA) supplied food for them; our supplies came from the US Army. The administration was in our hands. We had to file daily reports to receive our food rations. The camp could hold 250 people, but we often had double that number.

It took us a few days to get used to the new place, and we started our preparations for the big push. A man named Leon came from Ainring to show us the places where we would be able to cross into Germany. The border here was different than in Saint Valentin. We had to get the people across an international border between Austria and Germany. True, the Americans occupied both sides of the border, but they were different divisions. In 1945, the transports were permitted to enter Germany without any problems, but when the Americans discovered that the DP camps in Germany were getting filled up, the army closed the border. It was up to us to circumvent these restrictions.

One morning we took our truck and headed for the border. A man named Moritz drove Yojnale, Antek, Leon, and me close to the border. Moritz returned to Salzburg, to be back for a pickup in two hours. Our job: cross the border, walk to the nearest highway in Germany, and then return to Austria. A light snow had been falling all morning, but when we started to walk into the woods, it changed into a real snowstorm. We wanted to turn around, but Leon said that it didn't matter, because he knew the way. But it did matter. The wind was blowing the snow into our faces so hard that it was impossible to see even a few feet ahead of us. After half an hour of walking around in circles, we had to give up and return to the place where we'd been let off. We hid under an overpass and waited for Moritz to pick us up. The snow started to fall so heavily that it became a whiteout. Moritz somehow managed to find us, and we returned to Salzburg.

We had to sit for two days and wait for the storm to subside, but as soon as it stopped snowing, we started out again. This time, the truck took us close to the border checkpoint. We drove off the Autobahn onto a side road and started to walk into the woods. We met a farmer hauling a sledful of wood. For a pack of cigarettes, he directed us across the border into Germany. Around noon we came to Freilassing, the first railroad station in Germany. We boarded a train and arrived at Ainring.

If Hitler only knew.

Ainring had been the Führer's private airport. From here, he would go by car to his retreat high in the Alps, the Berchtesgaden. The Tyrolean-style villa where Hitler rested had been converted into a permanent DP camp. Now Jews who'd survived his death camps lived there. The barracks, where the airport crew had lived and where the repair shops had been located, were now occupied by our transit camp.

After hot tea and some food, we sat down to make plans for the future. We decided that every second night, we would bring a transport across the border to a prearranged location on the highway. Every time we delivered the people, we would set a new delivery time. Two trucks would wait at a prearranged point and take the transport away. They would wait one hour past the set time, and if we didn't show up, then they would return the following night.

We found our way back to Austria without any difficulty. Moritz was waiting for us. At camp Mülln, we were greeted like returning heroes. The planning of our first transport had started. I sat down with a man named Aba and a few of the other members for a planning session, during which we decided to send a transport of two hundred people. The idea was that if they caught a small transport of twenty, then we would be arrested for making an illegal border crossing, but two hundred people they would have to send back to camp Mülln.

The long-awaited night came at last.

The two hundred young boys and girls were loaded onto trucks and taken to the same place where we'd stopped on our reconnaissance trip. Everybody got off, and we started on our way. One truck was to wait for our return.

The night was cold and clear. The moon was shining, and the snow crunched under our feet. It reminded me that one year before, I'd been marching with other concentration camp inmates on a death march into Germany, surrounded by SS troopers. Now I was leading a transport back into Germany, and we knew where we were going: back home to Eretz Israel (the land of Israel).

We marched, staying in a single line so as not to show the border patrol—whom we were sure we would run into—how many people were among us. A song was going through my head:

> *Cu eins cvei, dray, cu eins cwei dray*
> *jeder trit hot zain klang*
> *gor an ander gezang*
> *wen du waist wohin du geist und wotcu.*

One, two, three
one, two, three
every step has its sound
and another song
when you know where you're going and for what
reason.

We crossed a narrow brook one hour later, and we were in Germany. After a short walk through a field, we found the trucks waiting for us, just as expected. We loaded the people onto the trucks, and they drove off. With our job done, Yojnale, Antek, and I, plus a few messengers, were on our way back. No problems. Back in camp Mülln, we went to bed for a long rest, while the people were being prepared for the next transport.

As planned, we took the second transport two nights later. Everything was going well until we arrived at the woods. There, a reception committee was waiting for us. We had left telltale signs during our last crossing, and now the Austrian border police and the American MPs were there.

I and the two other transport leaders slipped away into the woods, leaving a backup crew with the group. We were afraid that somebody might panic and point out the transport leaders. We had to walk about twenty miles to get back to camp Mülln, where we had to sit and wait for news.

Early in the morning, Eva (the Hungarian girl I'd become friendly with) came back. She was one of the transport helpers and had managed to escape from the barracks in which the MPs had locked up the transport people.

We received a phone call from the Americans at noon; they asked us to come and pick up a few refugees who'd tried to cross the border. We told them that we had no room for them, but after a while, we gave in and took the people into our camp.

That did not stop us.

We assembled another transport two nights later, and two hundred people found themselves in Germany. From then on, we kept changing the crossing times. We were going full steam ahead now, with two hundred men, women, and children in every transport. Many times we could see the sled tracks along the route we'd taken on our last trip.

One night after we'd left the trucks, a border guard tried to arrest Moritz the driver, but it turned out to be a blessing in disguise. Moritz took him to camp Mülln and made him an offer he could not refuse. He took the guard down to the food-supply room and showed him shelves loaded with cigarettes, sugar, coffee, and all kinds of preserved food. He gave him two alternatives: work with us, and you'll receive anything your heart desires, or we'll kill you.

From then on, whenever the guard was on duty, he would call on the phone to say that "Moishe" would see us tonight, and we would walk through the border under his escort. Once in a while, the American authorities gave us a permit for a transport, and we went by truck right into Ainring.

In February, the Austrian authorities started to furnish twelve-hour passes to people who lived in Salzburg and had to conduct business in Germany. The passes had a ten-kilometer limit, and the time of exit and entry was marked down. Some of our people obtained these permits, and we made good use of them. I often went to Germany and had to stay there for a few days, so in order to have my pass validated, another person with ID papers in my name would have to travel back to Salzburg. Making ID papers was never a problem. We had expert document forgers at every Brichah point.

One transport came from Vienna with a special passenger. A few people recognized a Hungarian SS man who was traveling with our transport as a Jew. He was put under a special escort, his possessions were confiscated, and we found half a pound of gold in his possession. It was a brick he'd stolen from the Hungarian National Bank. He was sent by special route to Ainring, and nobody ever heard from him again. The gold had to be taken to Germany to be sold. I was given the job.

We waited for a legal transport so that we'd minimize the chances of being caught. One evening, a legal transport of elderly people was put together, so I went with them. The gold was taped to my thigh, and because it was a legal transport, there was no inspection. The following day, I took a train to Munich, where the boys from the Brichah sold the gold for $850. With one part of my job done, the only thing left to do was to bring the money across the border to Austria.

Back in Ainring, we hid the money in a flashlight. European-style flashlights are flat, and we opened the wrapping of the battery and put the money in there; then everything was assembled again. The bulb was broken, so if they tested it, that would explain why it didn't work.

I started out after midnight, joined by a man named Bela and the transit worker Moniek I mentioned earlier. Newly fallen snow covered our pathway, and we soon lost our way. We could see the spotlights of the checkpoint in the distance. In our attempt to bypass it, we walked into a patrol.

"Händen hoch!" ("Hands up!") was their command, and we were soon surrounded by two German and two Austrian border guards. Inside the checkpoint, we had to undress, and all our belongings were examined. They handled and tested the flashlight a few times, but when I pointed to the broken bulb, they put it away and didn't look at it again.

We told them that we were going to Germany to look for family members. The Austrians were willing to let us go back to Salzburg, but the Germans would not budge. One of them told us that we had to wait until morning, when the Americans would arrive, and they would let us go. They said, "Don't worry! The commandant of this post is Jewish." I knew then that we were in trouble. I'd had some experience with a few Jewish American soldiers at the border in Mauthausen.

It happened when a transport had been stopped on the American side. I tried to get help from a group of soldiers, some of whom were Jewish—I called out in Yiddish, and a few answered—but they just walked away.

I was right!

The Americans arrived at nine o'clock in the morning and took us before their captain for questioning. "Why are you trying to go to Germany without a permit?" he asked. "You can be sent to jail for a year for that."

I told him that I'd just found out that a cousin of mine was an officer in the US Army; I'd tried to get a permit to go to Wasserburg, where he was stationed, but I waited in vain. Bela told him that he'd found out that his sisters had survived the concentration camps and now lived in Bergen-Belsen, and he also could not wait any longer. Nothing helped. The officer told us that we'd be taken back to Salzburg in the evening, when the soldiers returned home.

The border was opened for traffic around ten o'clock, and we managed to send a note to camp Mülln. Aba and a doctor came around noon and told us to keep calm and that everything had been fixed in Salzburg. They left us food and cigarettes and went back. In the late afternoon, when the soldiers returned to Salzburg, they put us on a truck and took us to the CID (the US Army Criminal Investigation Command). There we were interrogated again, our statements were taken down, and we were let go with a warning not to try any more illegal crossings. This was Friday, and on Saturday, we met one of the guards who'd caught us at the border. He recognized us and said, "I told you they'd let you go." He never knew how many strings we'd pulled to get ourselves out. The main thing was that the money was now safe in Austria.

CHAPTER 14

LOOKING FOR A NEW ROUTE

B y April, it had become harder and harder to get through the Salzburg-Ainring border, so we had to find a new route to get people out of Salzburg. Our eyes turned toward Innsbruck. Austria was divided into four zones of occupation. The Russian zone was Lower Austria, up to the River Enns. Upper Austria and Salzburg were in American hands, Styria and Graz belonged to the British, and Tirol (including Innsbruck) belonged to the French. Innsbruck was very important because of the city's proximity to the Brenner Pass, through which we sent our transports to Italy. The French occupation authorities were very helpful to our people, but from time to time, under the pressure of their British allies, they closed the border into their zone to us.

The French and Austrian patrols guarded all the railroad stations and often took our people off the trains. The highways, too, were watched, and many transports had to return to Saalfelden.

We had to find another way. One day, Moritz our truck driver, Bela and Antek, Dayka and Max (two other workers), and I boarded the train and went out to find a crossing into the French zone. There were two ways to get there. The long way was over a mountainous road around the tip of Germany, which abutted Austria. The other way was from Salzburg through the tip of German territory. The only problem was that we needed a transit permit to get across. The trip took one hour the short way compared to four to five hours the other way. We had to go the long way.

The roads were clear of snow, but the mountains looked beautiful, all white reaching into the clouds. We passed narrow, winding roads with high walls of rock on one side and deep abysses on the other. We drove in and out of so many tunnels that we lost count. We had breathtaking views down into deep valleys and up to the high peaks. But we hadn't come to enjoy the views. Our purpose was not to sightsee but to find a way into the French zone.

We eventually came to a spot where the map showed that the border was close. After we concealed the truck, we split up into two groups. Moritz, Max, and Dayka would walk along the railroad track until they came to a railroad station, where they would try to buy a ticket to Innsbruck. Bela, Antek, and I would try to find some way across the mountains into the French zone. After an hour of climbing up and sliding down, we had to give up. We came to the conclusion that we were not mountain climbers and that we had no equipment, and we had to consider the fact that the transports would include old people, women and children.

We continued our trek despite these setbacks and gave up only after I fell into a crevasse and was lucky not to have broken my leg. We sat down on the snow and slid all the way down a steep incline. Our clothing was wet, and we walked to the truck to wait for the others. It was getting dark by this point, and we started to worry if they had made it or if they had been arrested, and we wondered how long we would have to wait for them. After some deliberation, we decided to leave them a note on a tree where the truck was and go into town and find lodging for the night. Bela was the alternate driver, and he said to wait another hour before we left. The time was almost up and Bela was going to start the truck when we heard steps crunching in the snow and saw our companions.

They'd had no problems crossing the border, but the French had stopped them at the first railroad station. The soldiers gave them food and then escorted them back to the border, telling them not to try it again or they would be put into prison.

Moritz started the truck, and we took off on our way to Salzburg. After a few miles, Moritz gave us the bad news: we were low on gas, so we would have to try the short way, through Germany.

"But we don't have any permits to go that way," said Max. "The Americans will turn us back. Let's find a gas station instead and buy some gas."

"No good!" I replied. "We don't have any stamps, and nobody will sell us any gas without them, especially if they see that we're Jewish." Our truck had a large Star of David on the hood.

But Moritz won. Like they say, he was in the driver's seat. We asked a passerby how far it was to the German border, and he told us that it was not far. "A short way up that road," he said. We drove up a steep mountain road, praying that we wouldn't run out of gas before we made it to the top.

We made it, but we were stopped by the border police. The Americans told us to turn around and go back down.

"We ran out of gas!" we said. "We can't go anywhere. Give us some gas and send a jeep with an MP to escort us across to the Austrian side." But they wouldn't budge. "Please, call Salzburg," we said. "Get in touch with the military authorities and ask for Captain Nowinsky." The answer was still, "No!"

There was just no way to make them let us pass. All the soldiers and policemen came out of the post and started to push the truck until they'd turned it around, then they pushed us to the downgrade. The truck started to roll down. Moritz started the engine, but after a few miles it died on us. This time we really ran out of gas. We just coasted downhill until the truck came to a stop. It was past midnight now, and we were in the middle of nowhere. There was nothing to do but go to sleep.

We put some blankets on the windshield and doors, and our bedroom was ready. The six of us piled into the driver's cab and were asleep within a few minutes. It was early in the morning when traffic woke us up; we couldn't straighten out after spending the night in these cramped quarters. Imagine our surprise when we discovered that our truck was standing by a bridge on the other side of the village of Lofer.

We walked into an inn and had breakfast before finding a garage, but they wouldn't sell us any gas. A phone call to camp Mülln let them know what had happened to us. They promised an immediate gas delivery. We waited a whole day and called again, only to be informed that the jeep with the jerry cans of gas had returned to Salzburg, unable to locate us.

While we were stuck in Lofer, Moritz made a deal with the owner of the garage to overhaul the truck, so we had ourselves a two-day vacation. After two days, the work on the truck was finished, and the owner gave us a full tank of gas. We returned to Salzburg with the French zone still closed to us.

The group from Saalfelden eventually found a crossing, and we had to send the transports directly from Linz.

In order to save gas, the Americans sometimes gave us permits to take our transports from Salzburg to Saalfelden, going the short way through a good highway that traversed Germany near Bad Reichenhall. We had a travel-time limit of one hour from the point of entry to the exit. The time of entry was recorded on the permit and checked when exiting, which meant that we couldn't stop anywhere. During that hour, we made a side trip to our transit camp in Bad Reichenhall, where we took the people from the trucks off and put new people on. The whole plan was to take a certain amount of old people, women, and children to this transit camp and exchange them for young boys and girls who were destined for Italy and Israel. After the trucks got the young people in Saalfelden, the workers smuggled them to Innsbruck; from there they headed through the Brenner Pass in the Alps to the Italian ports, and then on to the illegal boats to Palestine.

This wasn't my territory, but I used to visit Bad Reichenhall very often; once I joined them for the ride. The trucks came from Austria and were rerouted into the camp. The exchange took place in a few minutes, and we were on our way again.

Of all the transports that passed this way, the one I was on happened to be followed by an MP. He watched the whole procedure and, after a few miles, stopped the trucks; he told us to turn around and follow him. The two transport leaders and I didn't wait until the trucks had stopped. They told me to follow them. As soon as the trucks passed some low-hanging branches, we grabbed the branches and held on until the trucks passed before jumping down and making our way back to camp. The transport was held for three days before being released. That did not stop us, though, and we started our job again after a few days.

As the saying goes, all work and no play, and so eventually we took some time off for relaxation. The best place for this was Bad Gastein, the most beautiful spot on earth I'd ever seen. The best hotel in town had been turned over to the Jewish Committee as a home for refugees.

The trip from Salzburg was an experience in itself. The railroad tracks ran over high mountains, through long tunnels, and over bridges spanning two mountains with deep valleys and narrow ridges;

I held on to my seat as I looked out the window. It seemed that the train was flying in the air.

The railroad station was located on top of a very high hill. The town of Bad Gastein is located in a deep valley, and we had to walk down into town. Surrounded by high mountains, it looked like a postcard. Hot water cascaded down the side of a snow-covered mountain right in the middle of town. The water, loaded with minerals, was piped into the hotel bathtubs. Fifteen minutes in a tub, and your body felt rejuvenated. We took rides on cable chairs and came back as often as we could.

CHAPTER 15

I'M IN LOVE AGAIN

One day, Antek and a woman named Ester came over and told me that Bela's two sisters were coming from Germany and that the older one would be just right for me. I was still single and didn't have a steady girl at the time, so I said OK. I thought, we'll see when she comes. She arrived, and I liked her from the first minute I saw her. She was a good-looking woman, healthy and in great shape. We soon became inseparable.

We met in the middle of April, and by May I was head over heels in love. This wasn't the first time I'd been in love, but this time we were together all the time, and I could not be without her for long. Many times while typing up lists of names for the transports, I had to leave my work to see her.

It was a short engagement. In June, Dorika (Dori) and I went to the courthouse and got married. Two of our friends gave us away, because neither of us had parents. We spent the honeymoon in Ainring and Bad Gastein. After the honeymoon, we moved into a small room on the upper floor at camp Mülln. But we weren't alone. The small room had three beds: one for Yojnale, the second one for a man named Abrasha, and the third one for us alone. We pulled a wire across the room and hung a curtain to separate our part from theirs.

After a few days, we discovered that this wasn't the best arrangement and were given a room of our own. It was not a room so much as a narrow, dark chamber with a long counter, over which the Franciscans had sold beer when Mülln had been a *Bierstube* (beer pub). We could only fit a single bed in there, so we had to sleep on our sides, nudging each other when one of us wanted to turn over.

We still weren't alone. Dori's younger sister Lili slept in our "bridal suite" on the beer counter. One day the management surprised us by giving us a normal room—with windows and a door that could be locked—of our own. We even had a closet where we could hang up our clothes.

Our work was starting to get easier. We became legal, but only on the Austrian side. The American command was only too happy to get rid of the refugees, so they gave us the necessary permits to cross the border into Germany. The Americans in Germany hardly welcomed them, however.

The transports left by train from the Salzburg railroad station, where the people were checked against our lists and stamped by the Austrian border police. When the train arrived in Freilassing, the Germans allowed the refugees off the train without any suspicion that something was not kosher.

The non-kosher part of the deal was that we had to create the lists of names and bring the list to the Americans for approval. By the time we got the papers back, three days had passed. In the meantime, the Vienna office kept sending people as soon as they arrived so that the flow from the east would not be stopped.

Not to be dependent on the Amis, we organized a few blank forms and made our own permits, using stamps made by a man named Marek, our expert stamp maker. By the time the authorities returned our papers, the people on the lists were long gone. That did not mean that we destroyed the permits. We used them for the new arrivals. We gave the new arrivals little slips of paper with names taken from the lists. We kept the new arrivals for twenty-four hours, or until they'd memorized their new names. It was just a precautionary measure, because the border guards at the railroad station very seldom checked our transports. They did occasionally search our people's belongings, just in case somebody was watching.

After a while, our relations with the guards became so friendly that they would allow the transports to pass on my say-so. They didn't do it because they were full of love for us. Every time we came with a transport, they told us, "Ich brauche Bohnenkaffee" or "Meine Frau möchte haben Zucker, Schokolade, Zigaretten." ("I need real coffee" or "My wife wants sugar, chocolate, and cigarettes.") A little note from me, and camp Mülln was ready with the goodies.

Very often my new wife would argue with me. "How come," she would ask, "when an Austrian asks you for something, you give him a note, but when I ask, you always send me to somebody else for a note?"

The road was open now, so we sent two transports a day—one by train, and another by truck. Despite all this movement, ever more and larger transports were arriving from Vienna all the time, so we were forced to open new transit camps. The situation in Poland had become unbearable. The pogrom in Kielce, where many Jews were killed, frightened a lot of people into leaving their homes and fleeing the country.

CHAPTER 16

MY NEW JOB

With the influx of new people from Poland, we were compelled to open new transit camps, where we would be able to keep them for longer periods of time. Franz-Joseph-Kaserne was the first new transit camp, which we renamed camp Herzel. Antek and I got the job of camp managers. This was an old Austrian military building with large rooms that was able to accommodate up to two thousand people. It was quite a change of a pace for us. From border smugglers we became office workers.

Our job was to requisition food, which meant making up daily reports and handing them over to the American supply officers. They insisted that we not make up reports with numbers ending in zero or five. We never knew the exact count, so we made up reports of 1,823 or 1,827 or 1,829 people and kept the same numbers, changing them only when an official transport left from or arrived at the camp.

The training we had did not prepare us for handling the situations we got into. When taking transports across the border, we'd dealt with people for short periods of time, and they were scared, so they listened to our orders. But now, while the refugees sat in the camp for longer periods of time, friction often erupted between the Polish and Hungarian Jews. The Hungarians felt discriminated against, so they kept sending Morci Batsi, the president of the Hungarian Jewish Committee, with all kinds of complaints. He fought for their rights.

Antek and I lived in camp Mülln and went to camp Herzel every morning to do our jobs. We had to make up transports and reports for food supplies, settle disputes, keep discipline, and other little things, like getting young people out of jail.

We had our own camp police and jail for our in-camp lawbreakers. Many boys got arrested in the city after being caught selling cigarettes on the black market. The girls, although it wasn't many of them, sometimes got picked up for soliciting in front of the soldier's club. And so it went on, day after day. Every day had new problems. I liked working the borders better, despite the dangers.

We had more time now, so we decided to have a real Jewish wedding. It was to be a double wedding. Dorika and I would be one couple, and some friends of ours named Metuka and Zev Helfant would be the other. On Sunday the eighteenth of August 1946, all the VIPs of the Brichah, the American officers, and all the people who resided in our camp took part in the wedding ceremony, which was officiated by a Hungarian rabbi in the garden of our camp. The rabbi had spent the war as a priest in a small Hungarian town, but after Hungary had been liberated, he became a rabbi again. Long tables covered with white linen were loaded with food, cakes, and plenty of wine. We had music and dancing, and there was no end to the horas. The fun lasted until very late at night.

The following day, I received a letter from America with the news that my cousin Meyer Tendler was with the US Army in Germany. I was very sorry that he could not be at my wedding. I was the only one without any relatives present at that most happy event in my life. Dorika had her brother Bela and his wife, Esti, and her two sisters, Lili and Monzi, the latter of whom had been brought back from Romania for the wedding. The other couple had family there, too. Zev's father and brother were there, and Metuka had two brothers at the wedding.

A week later, I went to Nuremberg, German where my cousin Meyer served as a dentist in a mil tary hospital. The meeting was very touching. Th last time we'd seen each other was in 1930, when h and his family had immigrated to America. Ther was no end to the questions. He wanted to know wha had happened to the whole family in Europe, and wanted to know all about everybody in America, e pecially Grandma. He assured me that she was we and that she hoped I would be able to go there whil she was still alive.

I invited him to come to Salzburg, but he tol me that it would be impossible for him to come t Austria. He could make it to Berchtesgaden, though and from there we would have to get him over t Austria. Before I left, we set a date when he woul come to see us.

On the day we were going to pick him up, we po ished Moritz's Buick and crossed over to German Meyer was waiting in front of the hotel in Hitler private villa, the Berchtesgaden. He would have t get a special permit to get into Austria, but with ou connections, we had no problems at the border. H spent the day with us, and in the evening we too him back. I went to see him very often after that. H often had packages the family had sent for me.

I remember once he had a dozen pair of tefi lin that Grandma had sent for me to give to ba mitzvahed boys in the camps. It was quite a large package, and I was sure I would have a problem at the border. I had to pass a border inspection when I left the train in Salzburg. When I opened the package, the inspector asked me what was in the boxes, and I told him that they were religious items. He took a knife and was ready to cut them open; only the intervention of an inspector who knew me stopped him from damaging the contents.

I now had a new job, so Antek took over management of camp Herzel by himself, and I was given a new camp. Camp Herzel was in operation until April 1947, when the Americans decided to shut it down. The people were ordered to move to another camp, but they refused to obey and blocked the doors. The army decided to remove them by force but failed. The soldiers used tear gas, but that also failed. When nothing helped, the soldiers went away, but they left a guard at the gate and shut off the water and electricity. The delivery of food by the Joint ended. Everybody who left or entered the camp was searched, and all food or water was confiscated. It was hard to believe that the Americans would behave in that manner toward the survivors of concentration camps. The situation at the camp became unbearable, and a hunger strike was declared at the Salzburg camps; after lengthy negotiations, we had to move our people to other camps. We could not fight the US Army.

CHAPTER 17

MOVING TO A NEW PLACE AND
A NEW JOB

Avalanches of people were now being sent to Salzburg. We had to open new camps: Bialik, an old army warehouse; Trumpeldor, an empty Nazi POW camp; and Jehuda, in Riedenburgkaserne, a former Yugoslav DP camp. The last one was my camp.

One day, Aba and Captain Nowinsky (both of whom I briefly mentioned earlier) picked me up in a jeep at camp Mülln, and we drove over to Riedenburgkaserne, where I was to be the manager. The camp had a two-story main building, a scattering of smaller buildings, and a few barracks, all surrounded by a high wall. The camp was empty and looked as if it had been hit by a tornado. Most of the bunk beds were smashed to pieces, and the straw used in the mattresses was strewn all over the rooms and hallways. Something else the previous inhabitants had left for us: bedbugs. Millions of them, crawling all over the walls, beds, and floors. We could hear the popping sounds when we stepped on them.

Captain Nowinsky got very angry, jumped into his jeep, and drove over to the camp where the Yugoslavs lived. He ordered them to come over and clean out Riedenburgkaserne. Every piece of wood and every bit of straw was brought out into the yard, soaked with gasoline, and set on fire. Then we brought cans of DDT and sprayed it over the entire camp. I came back every few days to check to see if the pests were still alive. It took two weeks until nothing was moving, and we declared the camp fit for human habitation. We installed new bunk beds and painted the walls and doors, and the camp soon looked new. With everything shining, we got ready to receive the first transport. Captain Nowinsky and I, joined by a few others, set out to acquire supplies for the camp. A Hungarian farmer sold us cabbage, carrots, potatoes, and other vegetables. Captain Nowinsky told me that this would make a good soup of at least a thousand calories per person. To this I answered, "Our people are used to eating bread and potatoes; they wouldn't know what to do with calories. We like full stomachs, even if there aren't any calories in them." So, he gave me a lesson about calories, to which I kept saying, "Yes!"—even though I didn't understand what it all meant at the time.

The camp was now open, and in no time it was filled with DPs. Our cook, Abraham, made up a crew for the kitchen to stay in the camp permanently. We obtained kitchen utensils from the US Army and were now ready for business. The police, under the leadership of a man named Lippa Skolski, kept order in the camp.

The rooms started to fill up with people. Large rooms accommodated a dozen families, and smaller rooms were for the camp management. I, as the camp manager, had a spacious room for Dori and me.

A few transports left regularly from each camp in Salzburg, but most of the camps became permanent settlements, where the residents waited for the day when Israel would be able to take them in as citizens.

The Brichah concentrated on younger people, sending them to Belgium, France, and Italy, loading them on boats, and trying to get them illegally to Palestine. Some of them made it, but most were caught and interned in prison camps in Cyprus. My sister-in-law Lili spent some time there, courtesy of the British government.

The year 1946 came to an end, and we wondered what 1947 would bring.

For us it brought an affidavit with an invitation from Uncle Izaak—my mother's brother—to come to America. We sent all the papers to the American consul and waited to be called for an interview. It was a big secret. The Brichah would've fired me immediately if they'd found out that we were not going to Israel. I wanted to go to the United States, because what was left of my family was there. The European branch of my family had been wiped out by the Nazis, and I wanted to be with relatives and feel that I was not alone. My grandmother, Uncle Izaak and his family, my father's two brothers, and a whole flock of cousins were there.

Israel was the country I had dreamed about for a long, long time. I had risked my life and liberty for two years while crossing the borders with various transports, but I yearned for the warm feeling of having close family nearby. I had nobody in Israel.

Time passed very slowly now while I waited for the call from the consul and dreaded being discovered and thrown out of the Brichah, which had been my temporary family for the past two years. This would have been a tragedy. They must have guessed something, because one day, Aba took me aside and proposed that I should go to Israel with Aliyah Bet, the code name for illegal immigrants to Palestine. I had to tell him the truth: I was going to America.

He was very upset and said to me, "One day when this is over, I intend to write a book about our work. I'll have to mention the names of all the people who worked with me. What will I write about a boy by the name of Siolek who helped to bring thousands of Jews to Israel, but he himself went to America?"

I had no answer to his question. Our minds were made up, and nothing anybody said would change things. The Brichah moved into a one-story building next to camp Jehuda, but Dorika and I worked and lived in the camp itself. Every once in a while, I took a trip to Nuremberg to see my cousin Meyer and return the packages my family kept sending from New York.

Time passed, and still nothing was happening with America. We found out that transports were now leaving from Germany, so we changed our address to Ainring, and Meyer wrote a letter to the American consul requesting a transfer of our papers to Germany. Now things were moving for us in both Austria and Germany. We wondered which would come through faster.

CHAPTER 18

THEN CAME TSEMACH

So he chased them out, and placed at the
east of the garden of Eden, Cherubims...

—*Genesis 3:24*

Tsemach was an Israeli who took over the Salzburg refugee point. He belonged to Hashomer, the left-wing party I mentioned earlier, and he initiated a lot of changes there: no individual ownership of things. Everything belongs to the whole group. All the clothing goes into one closet, for all to use. The workers did not like it, though, and they rebelled against his orders, and he had to give in. But in our case, he did not budge. In his eyes, I was a traitor, so I was relieved of all duties in the camp. He banned our entry into the Brichah building; we could no longer even take our meals there. I always pictured the scene of God evicting Adam and Eve from the Garden of Eden.

As in camp Herzel, life in camp Jehuda was tranquil during my term as administrator there. We always had a few problems with unruly people, but we straightened things out inside the camp. This incident happened after I'd left camp Jehuda.

There had always been anti-Semitism among the population of the city, and every once in a while, minor incidents occurred in which Jews were beaten up. This had never happened near one of our camps, though. One day, one of our people who was trying to get off the trolley bus at the stop next to camp Jehuda was pushed off by the conductor. The Jewish boy hit back. A crowd gathered, and when the bus tried to leave, somebody pulled the arm that connected the bus to the electric line. The Austrian police and the MPs were called, and the refugees ran into the camp. Our police prevented them from entering the camp, so they called in two tanks, ready for an assault on the camp.

The Austrians demanded that our police arrest the perpetrators and hand them over to them. Our police chief, Skolski, at first refused but eventually had to give in. As a result, he and four young people were arrested on suspicion of taking part in the rioting. Demonstrations broke out at all the camps, demanding that the arrested people be freed. Eventually they were conditionally released from prison, but our leaders had to promise that they would not attempt to leave. In order to appease the Austrians, the Americans put all the accused on trial. On March 25, 1947, the trial opened; Skolski was sentenced to six months, as were two of the others.

Without money, we had to depend on the camp food, which we were not used to. I couldn't go into the street and sell cigarettes on the black market, as so many of the others did. It was not in me to do so; besides, I was afraid to spoil my police record, since that would make it very difficult for me to enter the United States.

I'd once gone into partnership with a man who smuggled sugar into Austria, which he did very often without ever getting caught. Never, that is, except the one time when I was his partner. I lost my money in the adventure.

Another time, Abrasha (the one whom Dori and I had briefly shared a room with after our marriage) talked me into a deal. In Italy, the price of cigarette paper and knitting needles was very high. He traveled there almost every week, so we bought some merchandise, and guess what? Everything was taken away from him in Innsbruck by the men from the Brichah. I was a *shlimazl*. So that had been my last attempt to make a living in the black market.

By this time, the ORT (the Society for Manual Labor, named for its Russian abbreviation, Obshchestvo Ruchnogo Truda) had opened a trade school in our old camp Mülln. I enrolled in an auto mechanic class, and Dorika took a refresher course in dressmaking. After a while, she got a job as a dressmaking instructor and brought home a pay envelope once a month. A few months later, I got a job as a mechanic's helper at the UNRRA (United Nations Relief and Rehabilitation Administration) motor pool. With two pays, it became easier to survive.

At this point, Dorika's sister Monzi had met a fellow, and they'd both left for Israel; her sister Lili had been sent with a children's transport to Palestine but had been caught by the British and sent to Cyprus. Her brother had also left for Israel with his wife and baby. We were now alone. Soon the camp management started to demand that we give them back our room and move to a large room with other people. We couldn't get used to the idea of living in a communal room, though, so we started to look for a room in the city.

We rented a room from an Austrian widow on Mayburger Kay. We registered with the Jewish Committee, received our *Lebensmittel* cards (food stamps), and became residents of Salzburg. It felt good to be normal people again, living in an apartment, in a private house, and not a room in a camp with hundreds of other people. The view from our window of the Salzach River and the tree-lined boulevard, filled with benches to sit on in the evening, was a pleasure. No more waiting in line to wash up in the morning, take a shower, or just to go to the toilet.

Our landlady was a woman named Frau Schlegelhoffer, a widow with a young daughter. They had one bedroom, we had the other, and the unfinished bathroom was occupied by Herr Goralick, a Czech engineer who used to set up the sound equipment whenever Hitler made speeches. He was denazified, which meant that he no longer had the chance to kill any Jews. He shivered on his narrow army cot during the cold evenings. Other than being a former Nazi, he was a pleasant, intelligent man, and he taught us English in the evenings.

A couple of weeks after we moved in, our old friends the bedbugs showed up in our bed. We'd probably brought them over from Riedenburgkaserne, and it had taken a few weeks for the eggs to incubate. Can you imagine our embarrassment? I was sure our landlady was saying, "Die lausige Juden" ("die lousy Jews").

We had to bring a five-pound can of old reliable DDT, pile our belongings on the floor, and dust everything with the powder. We sealed the door and window and moved in with our new friend for a week. It took us a week to clean up the mess—no vacuum cleaners in those days. We got rid of the bedbugs and never saw them again.

And so we settled down, waiting every day for a call from the embassy, ready for our trip to the Goldene Medine, the Golden Land America. Then, in May 1948, the call finally came. We had to appear before the CID and fill out questionnaires, answering questions such as "Were you a Nazi?" and "Were you a communist?" with the repeated answer *No!* And so on, without end.

A month later, the consul called us in for an interview, and we were told to be ready to leave at any moment. We sat on our bundles the whole summer, ready to travel. In November, orders came for us to be ready in December. Meanwhile, most of our friends left for America or Israel.

And then came the long-awaited moment. The train left the Salzburg railroad station on its way to Bremerhaven and New York, taking Dorika with me to our new lives in America.

THE END

ABOUT THE AUTHOR

Saul Birnbaum was born in a small village in Poland before the outbreak of World War II. Like six million other Jews, he and his community were forced into concentration camps. Birnbaum escaped and joined the resistance.

After the war, Birnbaum immigrated to the United States with his wife Dora. They settled down in Brooklyn, New York, and raised two sons, Arthur and Howard. He wrote *A Witness to a Non-happening* as a defiant rebuttal to anyone who claims that the Holocaust didn't happen.

Huntsville Public Library
Huntsville, TX